Congratulations...
It's an Angel

The Gift of Talia

by Sandy Alemian-Goldberg

Published by: LifeCraft Publishing
PO Box 301
East Bridgewater, MA 02333

©1999 by Sandy Alemian-Goldberg
First Printing 1999
Printed in the United States of America

Illustration & Cover Design by Valley Graphics, Foxboro, MA
Interior Graphic Design by Synergistics, Norwell, MA
Printing by J&R Graphics, Hanover, MA

ISBN 0-9672065-0-2

Library of Congress Catalog Card Number: 99-62776

Acknowledgements

To Steve Viglione and Carol Hamblet Adams,
for their friendship and encouragement, and for being
role models as authors.

To Susan Desrocher,
for her helpful hints reviewing the manuscript.

To Jay and Tony Shippole,
for their talents in designing the interior of this book
(and also the Seeds of Hope ™ collection!)

To Helen and John Thompson at Valley Graphics,
for their beautiful job in capturing the essence of the book
when they illustrated and designed the cover.

To Michelle Constantino,
for helping me in the final moments, to tie up the visuals for
the journal concept.

To Linda Vanessa Hewitt,
for her loving editing, and her gentle "nudges" throughout the
process. Linda, you were like an angel unaware.

Dedications

To all the staff at Beth Israel Hospital, especially in the NICU, for helping us through our life's biggest challenge.

To *Claire Curran-Balquist*, for your wisdom and strength, and for your loving care of Talia.

To my best friends and soul-sisters, *Karen Paolino* and *Christy Serra*, for understanding me better than I understand myself sometimes.

To my best friends and real-life sisters, *Cindy Rice*, *Nancy Telian*, *Penny Castagnozzi*, and *Susie DeLuca*, for being my strength during a time in which I had little, for your shoulders on which I cried many times, and for taking care of Ariana during our challenging times. And especially to Susie, who was like a surrogate mother to Talia when I wasn't at the hospital.

To my parents, *Zarven* and *Roxy Alemian*, for your undying love throughout the years, and for still trying for a boy after four girls, and ending up with me!

To my little sweethearts, my children, *Ariana* and *Austin*, for being who you are, for making Mommy laugh, and for always reminding me what unconditional love is.

To my husband, my soul mate, *Rich*, for your unconditional love and support throughout our journey together. Thank you for allowing my soul to dance. I love you.

To *Talia*, my little angel, for allowing Mommy to know and love you, for leading me back to God, to my soul, and to my writing once again.

To God, the co-creator of this book, whose spirit filled me with courage, love, and insight during the many hours spent writing this book.

I wouldn't be who I am without all of you in my life. I love you all so much!

Congratulations... It's an Angel

by Sandy Alemian-Goldberg

Life is going to be challenging
and painful at times.
Instead of crumbling and feeling defeated,
we have a choice...
to learn and to move forward
with greater strength.

Preface

Some people
come into our lives and quickly go.

Some people
move our spirit to dance.
They awaken us to new understanding
with the passing whisper of their wisdom.

Some people
make the sky more beautiful to gaze upon.
They stay in our lives for a while,
leave footprints on our hearts,
and we are never, ever the same.

— Anonymous

*This book is dedicated to all parents
who are blessed with angelic footprints
on their hearts.*

A Note from Sandy

The following pages chronicle my journey through pain and loss into healing. I did not write this book alone, for I felt guided as I worked on the manuscript.

The messages in italics were divinely inspired by the Source of love and light, whom I refer to as God.

If only I could have heard them during the journey. My hope is that you will find strength, courage, and hope as you read these words. May they touch your heart and inspire you to reconnect with your sense of a higher power as your source of strength.

It is my sincere belief that a reawakening to our spiritual nature can provide the healing needed to move from pain to wholeness once again.

June 24th, 1995
3:29AM
Beth Israel Hospital, Boston, MA

Austin Louis Goldberg entered the world with a scowl on his face, a zesty cry from his lungs, and a thirst for life. Our lives had truly come full circle with the birth of this beautiful, healthy, little boy. What a gift straight from heaven! It was such a joyous moment for Rich and me, and we were both crying. These were tears of joy, but also of bittersweet memories of what had taken place at this very same hospital, exactly one year and one day earlier. How we had both grown, how different we were now. Our innocence was lost, but we had gained a deeper meaning for life. For it seemed like just yesterday that we heard the nurses exclaiming,

"Congratulations..."

It's *an angel.*

One

Day 1

This was the exact time and date of my next appointment with Dr. Hagen, but instead of meeting us at his office, he was delivering Talia Corinne! She was 12 days early, but it was certainly okay with us. One of my best friends, Karen, delivered her second child, a boy, last week. My other best friend, Christy, is about to deliver her first any day. It has been fun being pregnant at the same time. We've compared our cravings and the sizes of our stomachs and shared maternity clothes along the way. Yet just a couple of weeks ago, a fleeting yet still disturbing thought loomed in my mind. It would be horrible if something happened to one of our babies. It was hard to ignore a little pang that told me it was going to be mine. Swaddling Talia helped me dismiss that thought entirely. Welcome to the world, baby Talia!

> *How many times have you ever felt those little pangs, but ignored them completely? They are most often My way of trying to get you to pay attention to something. But you're often too busy to notice or too scared to listen to them.*

Talia weighed in at 6 lbs, 8 oz, the little peanut. She was so very quiet at birth, barely even making a sound when she was delivered. In fact it seemed almost too quiet in that small labor and delivery room. Talia also didn't want to nurse initially. But she scored well on the APGAR test (that measures vital signs at birth) so we felt at ease. Dr. Hagen explained that her quiet demeanor was most likely due to such a quick delivery (5½ hours) and Talia was probably just tired. We counted all her fingers and toes, and thanked God that she appeared to be perfectly healthy!

She was so cute, lying there with her hands clenched by her face, as if she was ready for a boxing match! It's never been easy for me to see who a newborn resembled. Talia is a beautiful baby with a full head of dark brown hair, which she gets from both Rich and me. Rich thought she looked like a combination of the two of us.

Physical beauty can be oh so deceiving. What meets the eye is such a tiny indication of what lies within.

This afternoon, Rich came back to visit with Ariana. Ari was bubbling over with excitement when she met her new little sister. Right from the start, she seemed completely enamored with Talia — as if she were a long lost buddy.

I was amazed at how big Ari looked (at only 2½) compared to little Talia. At home, we had been practicing with Ari and her dolly, Christina, how she needed to be gentle with a fragile newborn. It was so cute to see Ari's chubby little hands try to caress Talia *softly* — sometimes it worked, sometimes it didn't! As I watched this expression of love, a twinge of sadness teased my heart, as I realized that Ariana is no longer our little baby. She is now a big sister.

And a proud big sister she is. Ari was completely enthralled with her new playmate. She couldn't wait to give her the gift that she brought for her. It was a small, gray, stuffed dinosaur that Ari picked out all by herself at CVS. (We had no idea how important that dinosaur would later become to Talia.) Ari was surprised that Talia had a gift for her too. Rich snuck it into the hospital this afternoon. "Ooh, Mommy, look." she squealed with delight! "Talia got me a Fisher Price doctor's kit!" Ari never questioned where it came from. She just thought it was wonderful, and proceeded to take our blood pressure — under our arms!

> *Gifts appear to you in many different forms, and are not always ones that you can touch. Little do you know that Talia came bearing gifts for all of you, many of which you will come to appreciate much, much later.*

We've had other visitors today — my parents and some of my sisters. They brought new outfits and toys for Talia and took lots of pictures. Talia seemed nonchalant about the whole situation. She hadn't nursed and didn't want to wake up. She seemed content to rest and soak in all the attention.

Everyone commented on what an easy baby we have, because all she did was sleep. I wanted to take that as a compliment, but six hours after delivery, part of me wondered why she wasn't hungry at all. Oh well, I certainly was, and was eating enough for the two of us! Rich brought me some of the award-winning, homemade chocolate chip cookies from the hospital's cafeteria. Yum!

I was amazed at how good I felt — not like I'd just delivered a baby. And for whatever reason, I felt strange about that.

Later, some of our friends came to see the newest addition to our family. When I went to get Talia from the nursery, the nurses preferred that she not come back to my room with me. They said it was nothing to worry about. Talia was having a difficult time maintaining her body temperature, so they needed to keep her in the nursery. Okay, whatever was best for her. I wasn't concerned (alright, maybe I was a little). It was strange to have all this company in the room while something was missing from the picture. I was supposed to be bonding with Talia but I couldn't do it without her. I tried to keep a smile on my face, yet I wanted to cry.

As too many people do, Sandy. So often in life one feels sadness, but holds it inside, because of many lurking fears. Dear child, when will you learn to express how you really feel to those around you? Soon enough, soon enough.

This night, after everyone left, I started reflecting on all that Rich and I had been through in the last two years, all in preparation for the joy of Talia's birth. It seems as though so much growth was necessary to get us to this point.

In December of 1991, our first daughter, Ariana, was born at Goddard Hospital in Stoughton, MA, weighing 8 pounds, 9 ounces (which is why Talia looks like a little peanut!). She was a smiling and contented baby. Our little sweetheart was the joy of our lives. When Ari was 10 months old, quite to my surprise, I found out that I was pregnant again! After the initial excitement, I started to feel a sense of panic. A barrage of thoughts pounded in my head. Was Ari too young? Were we ready for another child? Could I handle two so close in age? Would I ever be able to balance my work and family? Soon, those fears decreased and I returned to the wonder and anticipation of a new baby with whom we would share our lives. But those confusing thoughts about family, about my ability as a mother, and especially about my career, made a permanent home in the deep crevices of my mind.

For the last three years I had been a partner in a sales firm in the toy industry. I loved the interaction with the buyers at our major accounts. My meetings with them usually took on a more personal tone. We'd talk about their families, their jobs, their challenges, etc. They trusted me. My partner Ray and I worked well together I had my office set up out of our house, and I managed to fit my work into a four-day week. But in all honesty, I didn't even like sales, with all its quotas, pressures, etc! And I was getting tired of all the driving within our New England territory. The position was lucrative, but it wasn't personally fulfilling.

In 1989, I had been trained to teach the 14-week Dale Carnegie course, a program that enhances public speaking and personal development skills. I taught this course one night per week. It didn't pay much, but it absolutely felt like my life's calling. Each course that I taught brought about an awareness of my deep longing to make more of a difference in the world. This type of work came so easily and naturally to me. I was passionate about motivating people to make positive changes in their lives, to begin to see the true potential within themselves. In 1993, I had contemplated leaving my sales career to become a professional speaker but I had a dilemma. Should I take a risk and follow my heart, so that I could truly help people? Or should I stay with what was painfully familiar to me, and follow the money that made me feel powerful and confident? How did a person make that kind of decision? I had not a clue.

> *They listen to their hearts, Sandy, although you aren't willing to learn this yet.*

Rich and I had talked it over, and decided that once this second baby came, I'd make that career switch and follow my heart. This plan sounded good and also bought me some time, something which I'm not proud to admit that I need when I'm not yet ready to make a decision.

Ten and a half weeks into this pregnancy, on December 30th, I was going out for dinner with my sisters. Staring into my closet, trying to find an outfit that still fit, I suddenly felt cramps. I ran to the bathroom. I had started spotting. Fear gripped me, so I stayed home and anxiously prayed, "God, please let this baby be okay." I wasn't sure if God remembered me, since I seemed to pray only when all else failed — when I was in a bind or was faced with a horribly scary situation. This was one of those times.

The next morning, the bleeding had worsened. My mother came over and drove me and Ariana to my doctor's office, which was about a mile from where Rich worked. Rich met me there, and my mother took Ariana home with her. The doctor on duty was the same one who had delivered Ariana. This time, I was too scared to exchange pleasantries. After a brief exam, he confirmed that I was miscarrying. A quick ultrasound showed that there was no fetus, just an empty sac. The bleeding was simply nature's way of expelling this pregnancy. The blood test had revealed that I was indeed pregnant, and my body had felt the effects of pregnancy. However, I was now informed that nothing had developed. I felt confused. How could this happen? I felt like a fool for having already told so many people that I was pregnant. I didn't want to face them. I didn't want to face anyone at this point. I just wanted to run and hide.

> *Sandy, you've done that all your life…you run and hide from issues that are not always so pleasant, that may involve a small amount of pain. Here is an opportunity to try it differently.*

After a D & C later that afternoon, they sent me home to rest. It was New Year's Eve, and there didn't seem to be much to celebrate. This miscarriage was a pathetic way to start the new year. I just hoped this wasn't setting the tone.

> *In time you will realize that you can bounce back from any challenging event with My help. Your soul knows that there is divine timing, but your mind does not know this yet. If you would only listen to My whispers in the callings of your heart and soul…instead of ruling with your ego.*

A couple of days later, I had a chance to speak to my own doctor. He chalked up this experience to "one of these things that just happen," explaining that approximately 30% of all pregnancies end in miscarriage. All of my four older sisters had kids (ten altogether), without miscarriages. My mother had one though; her first pregnancy ended early. She then went on to have five girls. She said it wasn't really a big deal back then. She just went on and tried again. So why was this so hard on me? Why did I feel so sad, like a part of me (that apparently wasn't even there in the first place) had died?

> *A part of you did die...the opportunity to follow the calling of your life's mission. But no need to worry, there will be other opportunities for you to see the path of light in your life, if you so choose. It is always your choice.*

As time went on and the sadness waned, I started accepting the miscarriage, telling myself that, since there was no fetus there initially, I really hadn't "lost" a baby. (I sometimes have a strange way of rationalizing things when I need to make sense of them.) As I reflected on my life, I realized that perhaps I was using this pregnancy as my ticket out of the sales career I felt stuck in. Now it was time to make a career move courageously on my own. Is this what I was supposed to be awakening to here? OUCH.

> *Reality can hurt when you have the courage to face it.*

I'd love to say that the decision was easy, that I just summoned up my courage and followed my heart, but it wasn't. In fact, I didn't do it. I rationalized that perhaps this *wasn't* the right time to make a career switch, that this miscarriage was a sign for me to stay right where I was and wait until we had our second child.

> *Somehow people see the signs they want to see and disregard all the rest that might serve them even better.*

In May of 1993, I went to my ob/gyn. Rich and I wanted to start trying to have another child and I hadn't gotten my period in a couple months. Irregular cycles were a part of my life, so this was no big deal to me. My doctor suggested that perhaps I was already pregnant. I knew that was impossible because I had just recently taken *two* home pregnancy tests (one the day before my appointment). Both were negative. Although he prescribed Provera, a drug that induces menstruation within 10 days, he said, "I strongly suggest that we give you another urine test to be sure that you're not pregnant." Did he not hear me? I had just taken one the day before! Irritated, I declined the test, especially since this appointment was now making me late for a sales call. Just give me the prescription and let me be on my way.

Impatience...lots of room for Sandy's growth potential.

Okay, so here was the plan (I just love plans — makes me feel like I have some sort of control).

Add control too.

Keep track of my temperature every day and take the prescribed pills. In ten days I'd begin my cycle, and then...well, Rich and I knew what to do from there. Day 10 went by and no cycle started. The next day, still nothing. My sister Susie convinced me to try yet another home pregnancy test. This time, that beautiful blue line showed up in the window, announcing with all its boldness that I was pregnant. How could that be? Half-confused and half-excited, I phoned Susie, who is a pharmacist. For some reason, she was a bit more restrained than I was when I told her my results. She explained that because I must have been already pregnant when I took the Provera, there were increased possibilities for fetal abnormalities. I suddenly felt sick to my stomach! How could this be happening? I called my doctor and he reassured me. "The chances are pretty slim that anything will happen. The drug companies *have* to put those warnings on the drug labels. Most likely, the baby will be just fine." I breathed a sigh of relief.

He seemed to be right. Nine weeks into the pregnancy, Rich went with me for an ultrasound. There, on the screen was the little "gummy-bear-like" shadow, heartbeat and all. We were ecstatic! It all made more sense now; the timing felt so right. On the way home that day, we were already beginning to make plans again for me to get out of my sales career, as soon as this second baby arrived. Aah, I liked the sound of this plan.

How often are people's lives continually pushed off...until that new promotion comes, until those last 20 pounds come off, until that right relationship comes along. Please don't wait. That time may never come.

Two weeks later, we were on our way to Disney World — Rich, Ariana, and me. An hour before we took off from Boston's Logan Airport, I began spotting the tiniest amount. Fear danced around my heart. How could this be happening again? Oh, God, please don't let me miscarry. Not now, not on our vacation. During the entire plane ride to Florida, I was a wreck. Ariana was thrilled to be on a plane, but it was hard for me to be fully present to share this experience with her. My mind was elsewhere. I tried to push the negative thoughts out of my mind, which was nearly impossible. It was ironic to think how often I had encouraged others to persevere with a positive attitude through challenges. Here I was struggling to fight back the tears, absolutely certain that I was losing this pregnancy. My own words started flowing back to my mind. "When faced with something out of your control, focus on something positive, and let go." Well, sometimes it's easier said than done. I didn't want to let go. I wanted this pregnancy.

Or did you want this pregnancy to be your ticket out?
Too many people wait to be saved by something or someone,
when all they need to do is trust themselves, follow their
hearts, and listen to that still, small voice that is always there.

Luckily, our vacation turned out better than it had begun. The spotting was ever so slight for a couple of days, then stopped completely. But I had to allow myself to feel the fear first, before I was able to calm down and convince myself that this baby was okay. We went on to have a wonderful time. We focused on Ariana's excitement at seeing all the characters and watched her splash and swim in the pool. When I allowed myself to stay in the present moment, my worry carried much less weight.

A few days after we returned from vacation, I had my regularly scheduled doctor's appointment. I was twelve weeks along. The nurse came into the examining room to take my blood pressure, and ask how I had been feeling. I told her about my spotting and she jotted down notes in my file. She didn't seem overly concerned. "Well, it's probably too early to even try, but let's see if we can hear this little guy's heartbeat," she said cheerfully. She put the heartbeat monitor on my tummy. I waited anxiously. We heard a lot of swishing sounds, but no distinct heartbeat. She moved the monitor around, trying to find something. I stared intently at her face, trying to see if I could detect any signs of fear in her eyes. She didn't seem upset at all. I, on the other hand, began to feel like I was going to cry or throw up. By the time she stopped, she could tell that I was scared. "Don't worry, Sandy, this happens all the time. It could be that we miscalculated your date of conception. Or perhaps it's because you're so small. We'll definitely hear it at your next appointment. I'm sorry that I tried so early." Well, so was I.

At that point, my doctor came into the room. He was brought up to speed on what had happened — the spotting, the lack of audible heartbeat. He calmly reassured me that I didn't need to worry; the spotting from the previous week was probably nothing. I trusted him and usually liked the way he fluffed off any concerns. But there was a feeling I couldn't shake. This appointment only added to my fear (or was it my instinct?) that perhaps something was wrong.

There's a subtle distinction between fear and instinct...fear
is an external unknowing...instinct is an internal knowing.

Just the next day, I realized how accurate our hunches can be. During a visit to my parent's house, the familiar scant traces of blood appeared once again. I immediately called my doctor. Knowing that he was dealing with "Nervous Nelly", he suggested that I come in for an ultrasound that afternoon to put an end to my fears. I called Rich at work. He insisted that he meet me there. Rich was always wonderfully supportive, rational, and kind, especially in times like these. I sensed he was also a bit scared, though he didn't show it.

While we waited for the technician to come into the ultra-sound room, I tried to brace myself for the worst possible case scenario. I heard a faint inner voice that gently whispered, "Sandy, you can handle this. No matter what, you will be okay." Still, my mind and my heart raced. And this roller-coaster ride was driving me nuts! I hoped the ride would slow down after this ultrasound. The procedure itself was getting to be too familiar — the johnny...the dim lights...that warm gel they squirt on your tummy. Rich and I squeezed each other's hands for mutual support. "Please, God, let there be a heartbeat," I repeated over and over in my mind. It seemed like it was all in slow motion as the technician moved the wand around on my stomach. The roller coaster made its way up the final hill — chug, chug, chug. Then the moment we'd been waiting for.... .

Well, the ride was in fact over, but with such sadness. Although the technicians are not supposed to share any details of the ultrasound (especially if it's bad news), we could clearly see that there was no heartbeat on the screen. She calmly said, "You can go over the results with your doctor." After we explained that we'd been through this before, and we knew there was no life there, she said, "I'm so sorry. It looks as though the fetus died one to two weeks ago."

Even though I had tried to prepare myself, it was still crushing to hear those words. Once again, I felt emptiness, confusion, and anger. I wanted to blame someone, as if that would take some of my pain away. I wanted to blame my doctor for prescribing the Provera. I wanted to blame myself for not taking that pregnancy test before I started taking the prescription. I wanted to blame God, for allowing that fetus to die. I was a good person! Why did these miscarriages have to happen to me? Was I not a good enough mother? Was that it? Since I'd never been one to express my anger outwardly, I held it in with all its toxicity. I felt like a complete failure.

> *No one is labeling you a failure, Sandy, except yourself.*
> *You are so often your own worst enemy, so quick to cast*
> *judgment on yourself. If you could just see yourself as I see*
> *you…a being of pure love and light. When you're ready…*

Summer that year brought healing moments. We spent many weekends playing with Ariana at Nantasket Beach, which was only about forty-five minutes from our home. I had heard the saying before that "time heals all wounds," and it really was true for us. It was becoming clear to me that pain can serve as a wonderful wake-up call. The one positive aspect to those painful miscarriages was that I began to reflect on my life from a different perspective. With a new level of awareness, I realized that I had to find courage within to make some changes in my life. I had to leave my comfort zone (or should I say *familiar* zone, because it wasn't all that comfortable), and step out into the unknown.

I finally did. But I took baby steps first. One day, a couple of weeks after my second miscarriage, I was sitting at our kitchen table having a cup of tea. I looked around the kitchen. Almond-colored wallpaper, linoleum, and curtains stared blandly back at me. There was no life to this kitchen! It was just dawning on me how drab our kitchen looked. Yuk! Rich was in the living room reading the paper. "Rich, I can't stand this kitchen, honey! We need more color in our lives!" He peeked out from his newspaper. The look on his face appeared to say, "Oh, oh, here she goes." (When I get excited about an idea, I have an abundance of energy, and I can't let go of the idea until I feel a sense of what to do with it.) Rich has never been that interested in the interior decoration of the house. That was left to my creative tastes. I wanted to start living my life in color!

Over the next few months, we painted the top half of the kitchen walls sea-green, and wallpapered the bottom half with a beautiful bright mixture of pink and green. I like to sew curtains, so I made valances to match our new color scheme. The valances also allowed more light into the kitchen. And we replaced our boring almond linoleum with pretty rose-colored tile. The boldness of the colors livened up the house and made me feel better emotionally.

Rich and I wanted to try for a second baby again, but I had some concerns that I'd miscarry again. My doctor said that one miscarriage was quite common and two were just plain bad luck. If I had a third, he'd run some tests to see if there was a reason for the recurring pattern. I didn't want to wait for the third one to happen. I went to a fertility specialist in Brookline, MA. My tests all came back normal, and in September of 1993, I was pregnant with Talia. The fertility specialist referred me to a new ob/gyn, Dr. Hagen, who was affiliated with Beth Israel Hospital. I felt that my life was back on track and moving forward.

The biggest leap forward came in January of 1994, when I was four months pregnant. I sold my share of the business to my partner, and gave up my sales career for good. I started teaching a ten-part self-esteem course that my friend Margot had developed. We taught it at different middle schools and I felt like I was finally on my path. What a difference a few changes can make. And all these changes stemmed from having two miscarriages. Okay, okay, so maybe there was some small silver lining to every cloud. It just seemed so dark in the moment when the clouds were ominous.

Remember, the darkest moments are right before the dawn of a new day.

Two

Day 2

Talia still wasn't nursing well at all and I was beginning to think that it was my fault. It has been two and a half years since I nursed Ariana, but nursing is supposed to just happen without trying so hard. Isn't it? I was still having a hard time just waking her up. We tried dressing and undressing her, tickling her — all those tricks they teach you in childbirth classes, but she wanted no part of any of it. She didn't really fuss either. She was just sleepy. The nurses were very reassuring. They told me that Talia was just tired and mucousy from a quick delivery. They said she'd be fine.

The young pediatrician on duty, whom I didn't know, came in, too. "Sometimes it takes babies a few days to catch onto this idea of nursing," she said. "She'll be alright even if she goes a few days without your milk. We can give her a little water from a bottle so she won't get dehydrated."

Sure, they were the experts, but I still felt concerned that she hadn't nursed yet. Part of my concern was that she isn't getting any nutrients, but a bigger part was that I felt she didn't even know or care that I am her mother.

She knows on a deeper level, Sandy, trust Me.

Talia spent the rest of the day in the room with me — the two of us catching up on our rest. Late this afternoon, one of the nurses noticed that Talia's head made some odd "twitching movements." After a consult with the head nurse, they sent Talia up here to the Neonatal Intensive Care Unit (NICU) to observe her overnight. Talia's little dinosaur tagged along with her so she wouldn't be alone. First her inability to nurse, then her unstable temperature, and now the NICU? Rich and I are becoming alarmed, but we can't possibly imagine anything wrong with our little Talia.

Often, the human mind "sees" what it wants to see and conveniently blocks out what it fears is real. Fear blocks one's vision; love and light dissolve fear.

The NICU is a whole different world compared to the maternity ward. Stepping off the elevator, one can immediately sense a heaviness in the air, as opposed to the joyous feeling downstairs. (Maybe it is my own fear I am feeling.) Before being allowed into the NICU, one has to check in with the receptionist. The nurse assigned to your baby's care is notified through an intercom system. The nurse then comes and brings you to your child's area. But before you can see your baby, you have to wash your hands carefully, adhering to strict sanitary precautions. Some of the babies here are fighting for their lives, and need no extra challenges with outside germs. There is a distinct smell to the NICU — a sweet, sterile smell that I eventually realize is from the antibacterial hand soap that is so frequently being used.

The noise level is a sharp contrast to the quiet bonding moments that are taking place downstairs. There are no babies crying...only beeping monitors and alarms, shouting to the world that this is serious business here. Initially Talia is placed in a rather open area with five or six other babies nearby. It doesn't have a cozy nursery feel to it. In fact, the openness makes me feel unprotected and vulnerable. The tiny semblance of atmosphere is created by the few rocking chairs they have and some pictures that were drawn by older siblings and taped to the walls of the isolettes. Other than that, there is an overwhelming presence of intricate equipment and wires. And tiny babies.

It is here, right by Talia's side, that I record my thoughts. I feel lucky that Talia is by far the largest baby in the NICU because she was full term. Most of the other babies here are under three pounds, and one of her neighbors is just over one pound. Our little angel doesn't look like she belongs here, nor do I want her here. I wonder if the other parents are envious of Talia's size. Surely their babies will have such a long road ahead of them; whereas Talia will probably be here just a day or two. Where do these parents find the courage to endure the obvious pain and heartache they must be facing every day?

> *What seems obvious to you may be just an illusion. You need to look beyond physical appearances in order to find truths — in any person and in any situation. You see abnormalities and automatically think suffering, as if there is only one way to see it. To address your question about where they find courage… many who heal themselves and have inner peace do so through Me, the Creator of love and light, though you are not familiar with that…yet.*

Later tonight, they observe Talia having several mild seizures. The doctors have no explanation for us, although they say that seizures in newborns are not uncommon. Okay, so quickly figure out what's causing them, and let us go home and be a family.

> *Patience, patience…you are in such a hurry to fix whatever hurts. If you would just have faith in the Divine plan, you would trust that I have your highest interest in mind…in all ways for always. Many never reach their ultimate heights, though, because they do not let Me lead the way.*

My real room is still downstairs in the maternity ward. I don't want to go back there. I want to stay right here by Talia's side. Reluctantly, I went back for a while to get some sleep. Several times through the night though, the NICU nurses called me to come back up here to see if Talia would nurse. I was excited and ready to try again, but Talia couldn't, or didn't want to. I feel frustrated, like I am failing as her mother. She can't really get the grasp of sucking from a bottle either, but I still feel rejected by her.

If you would just turn to Me, dear one, I never have and never will reject you. LOOK TO ME.

Day 3

June 25

Today is going to be our discharge date. Well, it is for me, but not for Talia. What a horribly empty feeling.

In the hospital lobby, it was incredibly painful to see other new mothers being discharged with little babies swaddled in their arms. They all looked blissfully happy, and I was sad and angry that Talia wasn't coming home with us. Rich kept trying to reassure me that Talia would be fine and that she'd be home soon. I'm not convinced. I'm scared. Desperation and panic settled around my heart.

I need to blame someone for the unfairness of all this. My initial target is God. "God, why is this happening? This is not fair!"

When in pain and out of control, many choose to place the blame on Me. You have far greater power of choice than you realize. My child, know that whether it is an angry demand, or a silent prayer, I hear you always. You are never offered an experience without first the tools with which to handle it. Trust that you will grow through this. When you so decide, you will hear these words within your heart, and start to believe them. But I cannot help you until you first ask for help.

When we got home, the house was eerily quiet. Ariana was at my parents' house. I walked down the hall to Talia's nursery and felt as if a part of me was missing. Her room cried out for her. The glider remained motionless, waiting to offer comfort at nap-time. Her stuffed animals sat prettily in her crib, waiting to be snuggled and drooled upon. The Fisher Price monitor's red light was ready, waiting to alert us of her cries. Everything in this room was put on hold, just like our life.

Day 4

June 26

The nurses sent me home yesterday with one of Talia's receiving blankets that smells just like her. They explained that it would help me to continue to express my breast milk so I can nurse her when she gets home. I like the sound of that — not *if*, but *when* she gets home.

Early this morning, at around 1:00AM, I woke up and my heart ached for Talia. It felt so unnatural to be at home without her. I ran to get her blanket and nuzzled my face in it, breathing in her adorable newborn smell. It was more than I could bear. The searing pain burrowed holes right through to my soul. I went into the bathroom hugging her blanket, collapsed to my knees on the floor, and sobbed uncontrollably. "How am I ever going to make it through this crisis in one piece?"

Part of me felt like I was going crazy with sadness and rage. And whatever was left of me felt totally empty inside, as if the very life energy was slowly draining right from me. At other points in my life, I remember feeling depressed or hopeless, but never that low physically, emotionally, or spiritually.

I doubted that I'd have the strength to handle this. I was way over my head, and needed help. Not knowing what other choice I had, as a last resort, I pleaded with God, "*Please, please, please*, dear God, help me!!!" Could God even hear me? How would I ever know?

> *You've felt the pain, frustration, desperation, and have now cried out for help. It matters not when or how one cries out for help; what matters is that you turn to Me. Open your heart so that I may enter.*

My sobs must have awakened Rich because he came into the bathroom a few moments later, worried about his hysterical, postpartum wife. He kept reassuring me that Talia would be all right. I desperately wanted to believe him, but I had too many questions left unanswered. Rich gently walked me back to bed. I listened to his breathing slowly become more rhythmic until he fell back to sleep. I, on the other hand, laid there awake, feeling exhausted, reflecting on how, in only three short days, our lives had been turned upside down. At that point, all I wanted was a small thread of hope that I could cling to for the night.

*There is always hope to hold on to — perhaps not always
for physical healing, but there always remains hope for
spiritual healing. I feel your sadness always. It saddens
Me that you allow yourself to feel so much pain before
turning to Me.*

I certainly thought I could handle this on my own, but now I was way over my head, in crisis mode. I'd read before that when some people prayed, they instantly felt like they were surrounded by a warm glow of love. I began *pleading*, "God, if you do exist, you've got to help me get through this night — I can't take how much this hurts! *Please*, dear God, let Talia be okay." Why is it that I wait for some crisis to turn to prayer?

I experienced no warm glow. Nothing, except for the burning pain in my heart, and the massive headache from crying so much. Did my words of prayer just dissipate into the darkness? I had no idea. I'd always wanted to believe that there was someone or something listening to my pleas for help, but I really had no proof that God existed.

*Your ego needs proof. Your soul does not. Open your
eyes and see; open your ears and listen; open your heart
and believe.*

At some point during the stillness of the early morning, the ache in my heart began to fade, and I drifted back to sleep.

Three

Perhaps my uncertainty about God stemmed from my childhood. I remember my mother telling us that God watched over us all the time, but I can't remember feeling like there was a strong connection there for me. My earliest memories of religion were of going to a musty-smelling Sunday School at a Methodist church in Weymouth, Massachusetts. But I never paid much attention. The lessons didn't hold my interest, and I saw no importance in having to memorize all the chapter names from the Bible. "Matthew, Mark, Luke, John...," that's about as far as I got.

As kids, we faithfully said our prayers in bed every night. "Now I lay me down to sleep...may the angels watch over me...," and " God bless Mommy, Daddy, Cindy, Nancy, Penny, Susie (my older sisters), and Herman (our miniature Schnauzer)..." were the standard prayers. I also remember many a night, tearfully pleading with God, "Pleeeeeease don't let anything ever happen to Mommy and Daddy." Both my parents were perfectly healthy, but I was scared nonetheless. I could never bear the thought of losing anyone close to me.

As time went on, prayer for me was increasingly like going through the motions, reciting words without much meaning behind them. That was, until I was in junior high school, when it became a little more personal. My most vivid prayer memories were lying in bed at night, once again pleading with God that

He make me skinny (I was a tad chubby as a child); or that He'd make Jason, John, or Larry (whoever was the subject of my latest crush) fall in love with me overnight. God never did answer *those* pleas…maybe that's why I gave up on praying. I figured I wasn't worthy, or that I wasn't doing it right. I guess my image of God was of some man in a white robe who sat up in heaven, granting wishes to you here and there, if you were lucky.

Sometimes My greatest gifts are unanswered prayers.

In high school, my parents took us to the First Armenian Church in Belmont, about 40 minutes from our house in Weymouth. The trip seemed like an eternity. Inevitably, one of us kids would complain of feeling carsick! Half the service was spoken in Armenian (of which I understood only a word or two), so I was bored silly during the entire hour and a half. I'd usually end up writing notes back and forth to my sisters. We'd start laughing uncontrollably (you know how it is in those most inappropriate circumstances, when the harder you try to stop, the more you start to snort?!). Needless to say, as I grew older, religion was not a top priority for me, and I was turned off by anyone who seemed to be a religious freak or tried to force me to understand something in which I had no interest.

In my late twenties, however, I faced darker times, when I felt overwhelmingly powerless or frustrated. Out of sheer desperation, my soul called out to God, and asked for help to get me through whatever "blues" I was experiencing. One such time was in December of 1988, during a rocky point in my marriage. Rich and I had met at Bryant College in Rhode Island in 1980, when I was a freshman and he was a sophomore. We had mutual friends and we all played on the same intramural co-ed volleyball team. I gave him and his friends haircuts in my dorm suite — my way of earning spending money in college. I didn't have any formal haircutting experience. I always watched my mother cut my father's hair at home, and I used to cut my own hair on occasion. Pull up the hair, measure it to a certain length on my finger, then snip! Rich was always one of my best tippers.

I was attracted to him physically, with his dark curly hair and his beautiful blue eyes. But I also admired his always easy going nature. Rich had a way of making people feel comfortable around him. And he always knew how to make me laugh. I always felt he brought out the best in me. In March of 1981, we started dating and got married in August of 1985. Though neither of us was strong in our faith, because of our different faith backgrounds — Rich was raised Jewish and I was raised Protestant — we had our wedding ceremony and reception in a restaurant's function hall. Our family's Armenian minister along with a "traveling Rabbi" we found from New Hampshire officiated at the ceremony. We combined the two cultures in that beautiful service. And at the reception, 150 guests happily celebrated the beginning of our new life together, dancing part of the night to the unique sounds of an Armenian band, and the rest of the night to the music of a traditional band. Our honeymoon in Aruba was a tropical paradise…a perfect way to begin our journey together. If only life could stay that easy.

By 1987, Rich and I were both on the fast track in our careers. I was a toy buyer for Child World/Children's Palace, a toy chain with 183 stores. Rich was the assistant controller for a large convenience store chain. We both worked long hours and had considerable stress in our jobs. Our marriage wasn't turbulent by any means. In fact, we hardly argued. (Maybe that was part of the problem!) We were like two ships, though, sailing off in different directions. To others, we appeared to be a happy couple. But in reality, I hadn't been happy for some time. My self-worth had always been based on my appearance, status, and achievements (all external influences). My happiness was tied to everything ego-driven: compliments about my looks, raises at work, the glitz and glamour of being wined and dined by the salespeople who called on me. When that ego rush wasn't there, I felt less than whole. I didn't know who I was. Rich was as sweet as ever, but I blamed him for my frustrations though I never verbalized them. I realize now that my own lack of inner confidence had created a deep need for approval and acceptance from the outside world. There was no way Rich could fill that void and I didn't know how to be entirely truthful with him about my feelings. Why was it hard for me to communicate to him what I needed? Once again I felt stuck.

On Christmas Eve that year, I was in deep despair. My marriage was crumbling. I didn't know how to pick up the pieces or even discern which pieces fit anymore. I decided to go to the 5:30 holiday service at a local church, hoping to find some solace. Rich had no interest in church, so I went alone while he stayed home. I was surrounded by apparently joyous couples with their children, all dressed up for the holiday. I felt pathetic being there by myself, and started feeling more sorry for myself. After the service, I drove to a vacant Papa Gino's parking lot on the way home. For the next half hour, I cried from the depths of my soul. In the solitude of my car, I let down my stubborn barriers and prayed for help. "I need help, God. I'm so confused about what to do. I don't know how to sort through these feelings I have inside of me. I don't even know *what* I feel anymore. Please help me!"

Did God hear me that night? I didn't know, but, I had an interesting spiritual experience early one morning about a week later. I was in that in-between state of not being entirely awake, but not being entirely asleep either. Suddenly, a large sphere of white light came towards me, and I sensed that it was sent by my friend Lynn, who, at that time, was the only friend I had who was spiritual. As this white light got closer, it got bigger and brighter and whiter! I instinctively knew that whatever it was, it was powerful. I knew I had to position myself so I would be embraced by it. This white light struck me with such a force that I immediately opened my eyes, had chills up and down my body. The message in my mind was loud and clear,

"I now have the power to do anything I want in my life." I didn't quite know what to make of that experience, but something in my soul had shifted.

In January of 1988, one month after that vision of white light, Rich and I began marriage counseling. In February, we decided to separate. If we were ever going to make it together, we sensed we first needed time apart. It felt as if I were going through a mid-life crisis at 26 years of age. Though we knew that this was the best decision for both of us, it was nonetheless a painful one. A separation seemed so final. Was this the right decision? Over and over again, I questioned it. My mind offered no definitive answer.

I offered to move out, since I felt this mess was all my fault. I had caused Rich so much hurt, because he couldn't understand how I was feeling. Neither could I many times. I loved him, and he was a sweet, kind, and intelligent person, but something was missing from our relationship. Rich and I had moved into this brand new four bedroom house only a year earlier. We had such plans for our future when we first moved in. Plans that definitely included lots of children someday. Plans that would have to be held in our hearts, waiting for a chance to see the light — someday.

Moving day was a dreary, rainy Saturday. Rich had decided to visit his family in Connecticut for the entire weekend so we wouldn't feel the excruciating pain of saying good-bye to each other. We still loved each other. My brother-in-law Richard came over with a pickup truck to help me move my things. I wasn't taking much — my clothes, toiletries, essential kitchen items, and some pictures. I remember walking through our home, room by room, with a heavy heart. Trying to absorb any last minute memories to store in my heart, I stopped to look at our wedding portrait on the living room wall. We looked like two innocent kids — our eyes sparkling with bright hopes for the future. Tears fell as I bid my final good-byes to this home of ours. As I drove out of our long driveway, I glanced over at the apple, plum, and peach trees my father had planted for us the previous year. "Sandy," he'd said, "in a few years when you kids have children of your own, these trees will be ready to bear a lot of fruit for you all to enjoy." I had no idea if we would ever see that day.

I drove away from our quiet suburban neighborhood and cried the entire 35 minute drive to Weymouth, to my new "home" — an apartment complex about ten minutes from my parents' house. My tiny, one-bedroom basement apartment was a far cry from our contemporary lofted raised ranch. I borrowed an old green couch, a TV, and a double bed from various family members and created a makeshift living space that would be my home for an indefinite amount of time. In the still of the night, I could hear the upstairs tenants shuffling around and the cars driving by outside. Life was going on around me, and I was more confused than ever. I was scared to be alone. I'd never lived on my own — except at college, and even then I had six roommates in our dorm suite. But this was my choice, and I had to live with it. I cried myself to sleep many nights. What was I doing with my life? Where was it all heading? Was I throwing away the best thing in my life? I didn't have a clue and that frightened me. As I went to bed each night, I prayed, "God, if we are meant to be together, help us work this out."

During that painful time of separation, I grew spiritually. I started going to church on a more regular basis. It brought me inner peace and helped me feel reconnected to God. I began reading spiritually nurturing books that explained that there was a purpose to the challenges and pain we face in life. Rich and I continued with marriage counseling. I learned how to communicate what I really felt, and I began to realize that my self-worth was tied to other people's perceptions of me. I needed to look within to find my own happiness. Rich had encouraged me to see it that way all along. Fortunately, he allowed me to come to the understanding on my own. That's unconditional love, when others allow us to grow at our own pace, rather than their pace. I realized how right he'd been and was thankful for his insight. I started seeing him through different eyes. For the first time in a long time, I truly appreciated all his wonderful qualities. Happily, we reconciled after three months of separation. I guess we were meant to be together.

Rich and I went on a second honeymoon to San Francisco. One week after we returned, I was enrolled in a powerful 14 week Dale Carnegie course (for self development and public speaking). I would go on to teach that same course for five years. I started seeing myself in a different light. All through my teen years, I had compared myself to my older sisters. There were nine years difference between Cindy, the oldest, and me. We looked a lot alike — dark hair, dark eyes, and all varied in height from 5' to 5'4". I always wished I was more like them because I saw them as prettier, funnier, and more musically inclined and artistic than I. In my mind, I never quite measured up. And it's funny to talk with them today about those childhood feelings. They felt the same way about themselves. Although everyone may go through that stage, mine felt more like a way of life until I took the Dale Carnegie course. It encouraged me to look inward to my own strengths, rather than focusing on the qualities I didn't have. I realized that I had a gift for speaking in front of a group. It was a gift that had been waiting patiently to be opened, whenever I chose to recognize it.

I also sensed that on some level, perhaps I had been afraid that if Rich really knew me, he might not love the part within me that I deemed unlovable. But joy was blooming in my heart. I began to like who I was from the inside out and felt connected to my soul. I felt like my life was just beginning. Did God really hear my crying out for help on that dark December night? Maybe it was all just a coincidence.

*Not only do I hear you, I am always responding.
Coincidences are not merely chance happenings, they are
My answers to your prayers. Your job is to simply be open
to them. Please know that once you rediscover love from
within, you can truly see the beauty of life. Remember that
each one of you has special gifts. And you all have one gift
that is the same…the inner beauty of your soul. Make the
connection.*

Day 5

June 27

It's so much easier to see the patchwork design to our lives
when we're on the other side of pain. Right now, I'm not on the
other side. I'm right in the middle of it, and I can't see a thing.
Talia was placed on a respirator today because her breathing
was erratic. I desperately need strength to deal with our very
sick child, but all I can feel is the pain. If I really was connected
to God's presence what seems like a lifetime ago, why can't I
feel that connection now? How can it be so easy to lose that
spiritual connection? Why isn't God answering my prayers now?

*I am answering. You never really lost the connection, you
have merely chosen not to see and hear My responses. Fear
has taken My place. Open your heart, listen to your soul,
and trust that I am here.*

Four

Day 6

June 28

The doctors in the NICU now begin the process of trying to pinpoint the cause of Talia's seizures. She is first put on Phenobarbital to stop the seizures, with the level of medication gradually increasing each day if she has more seizures. She is hooked up to an IV through which she receives her medication; she has a tube in her nose through which they feed her; and she has several other monitors on her. Yet even with all her little tubes and wires, Talia still looks absolutely beautiful, with her fuzzy, brown, curly hair, and her hairy little shoulders and back. Although the Phenobarbital makes her lethargic, she is nearly seizure-free. This must mean she'll be home soon!

Yes, dear one, she will be home soon.

Because they still have no firm diagnosis for Talia, they're testing her blood for close to 200 different disorders. In addition, she has had a CAT scan, an MRI, a spinal tap, and an EEG. I am here for almost all her tests. When I'm not, her gray dinosaur goes with her for protection. It sounds so silly, but we feel as if this $1.99 dinosaur is like a little guardian angel for her. I wish I knew if there really are guardian angels. We sure need one here.

Remember your prayers as a child. "May the angels watch over me…" If you would only open yourself to feel the comfort of the angels around all of you now, you would realize that you are never, ever alone.

The procedure that is the most difficult for me to watch is the electroencephalogram (EEG), which measures patterns of brain waves. It determines the functionality of Talia's brain. Although the technician assures me that the procedure won't hurt, I grow more and more anxious as she glues each tiny electrode onto Talia's little head. Talia's fate is about to be determined and she looks defenseless.

"Please God, let her brain be normal," I chant silently. With tears streaming down my face, I visualize sending Talia white light, surrounding her whole body. I don't know what I am doing or if I am doing it right. I remember that white light "dream" and sense that it may have stood for healing energy. My heart is telling me that, if I pray hard enough for God to make her well and send all of my positive energy to her, she'll be okay.

Yes, dear one, she will be okay.

Well, maybe not. The EEG results show that Talia's brain is indeed seizing. The bad news is that following the seizures, there is no normal brain activity. In essence, there is just a jumbled mess of electrical activity happening inside her brain. Either the results are thrown off by the fact that she had a seizure during the procedure or her brain is so damaged that it is not capable of sending proper instructions to the rest of her body. Before the doctors commit to any formal conclusions, they want to repeat the EEG in a couple of days to compare the readings.

They tried to take her off the respirator a few times over the last couple of days, the last to see if she could breathe on her own. She did for a while, then had periodic episodes where she didn't breathe in deeply enough. They put her back on the respirator, especially since she had brief periods of turning dusky in color. Thank God I wasn't here in those moments to see that.

*You're welcome. Is the light finally dawning that you do not
need to endure this pain alone — you now mention My
name, yet do you truly believe that all will be okay if left to
the loving Creator? Let go and let Me enter your heart.*

Day 7

June 29

So far, all of Talia's test results are coming back normal,
except for that dreaded EEG. It is repeated this afternoon, with
the hope of seeing some improvement in the results, of seeing
some normalcy in the patterns. Yet it reflects no changes at all,
just the same abnormal brain waves. This is not a good sign. In
addition, her neurophysical exams are grossly abnormal-no
suck reflex, no grasp reflex. C'mon, Talia, you've got to help us
out here! "C'mon, God, you've got to help *her!*"

*Sandy, she needs no help from Me...you do. I have been
here with you all along, waiting.*

Day 8

June30

More seizures in the middle of last night — three in one
shift. Talia is lethargic and rarely opens her eyes. Her level of
Phenobarbital is so high now that it has put her into a coma.

Some of the nurses have given her the nickname, Sleeping Beauty, which describes her perfectly. Despite the swelling in her face, arms, and legs from the medication and all the poking and prodding, Talia has an astounding beauty that seems to radiate from within.

Aah, perhaps you are getting it now…

And the good news for the day (or so I thought) is that because she is under so much sedation, she is seizure-free! Well, at least I think it is a good sign. That is our ultimate goal, for her to be seizure-free so she can come home with us. I always tend to hold on to any good news. And now, any hope at all keeps us going moment by moment, waiting for our miracle.

*Perhaps your little Talia **is** a miracle **as she is**. Why is it that many wait all their lifetime to see a miracle that has been right in front of them all along?*

Most of my waiting moments are spent right here by her isolette in the NICU. I stroke her hair, nuzzle her face, tell her to be strong, and sing gently to her. "You are my sunshine, my only sunshine, you make me happy when skies are gray. You'll never know, dear, how much I love you. Please don't take my sunshine away." All the while, tears softly roll down my cheeks. With every passing moment, it feels as though the sunshine in my life is fading.

Allow your heart to be filled with My love and light. You have My promise that it will never fade.

Though terrifying pain is ever present in my heart, there are mystifying breakthroughs. It is as if the heavens open up after a raging storm, delivering gifts of calmness and inner strength. These odd, yet wonderful, moments are accompanied by an intuitive sense that all will be well, no matter what happens. I don't know how to explain the feeling to anyone, it just surfaces from within. However, in an instant, from out of nowhere, a massive undercurrent of fear too easily sweeps away that gift of peace and strength. Since fear is the dominant force in my heart, my hope is eroding. For four days — what seems like a lifetime — I haven't been able to hold her, rock with her, change her, or do any of the motherly things I am supposed to be doing for her. My daughter is lying here lifeless, without a good explanation, and I have no way to help her.

You may not have control, but you always have a choice...you have been afraid to ask.

The uncertainty of Talia's diagnosis horrifies me. Although I am ashamed to admit it, I think I am terrified of getting emotionally attached to Talia. How would Rich and I survive if anything happens to her — how would we endure that kind of pain? Am I secretly relieved that all her apparatus serves as a barricade between us, a fortress that shields us from pain? Wouldn't it be easier if I protect my heart? Oh my God! How can I possibly think these thoughts? Talia is my daughter! Well, the thoughts are here, lurking in the dark corners of my mind, and they scare the hell out of me.

Many choose to go through life hiding their hearts behind walls of varying heights. Depending on the level of pain in one's life, those barriers can be progressively tougher and tougher to scale, making the journey back to the heart a very uncomfortable process. So many choose to run from this process in their own unique way — over-drinking, overeating, overworking — any conceivable way to numb their pain. Ultimately, they never reach the emotional intimacy that their souls long for, and they spend their waking moments in their own hell, trying to find their way out. The ability to walk a path to inner peace even through painful events is up to the individual. I can help ease the pain, the suffering, the trauma, and even offer hope beyond the pain. Trust is the key. But for now, little one, concentrate on your precious angel before you...and what she is here to teach you.

Our favorite nurse, Claire, was on duty this afternoon. Claire has no children but has seemed to bond closely with Talia and with us, too. I vent my feelings to Claire — the good, the bad, and the ugly! She is becoming like a sister to me. She listens to all my confused emotions and seems to understand completely.

"Sandy, whenever you feel ready, you can start to get more involved with Talia's daily care — changing her diaper, or taking her temperature in order to feel a closer bond," Claire says.

"Could we start slowly, Claire?" My fear wants to hold me back, but my heart tells me to go for it.

Ah, at long last, you will now be able to slowly face your pain in order to grow through it.

The first thing we try is a technique of holding Talia, called "kangaroo-ing." To do it, I have to first lay on a recliner, wearing a hospital johnny that is open in the front. Claire then unhooks Talia from her ventilator, places her on my bare chest, and quickly reconnects her, hoping that Talia doesn't get too distressed during the process. I was nervous that she would stop breathing or that she'd have a seizure while I held her; Claire reassured me we'd both be fine. She was right. Within seconds, Talia's warm, still body is placed upon my bare skin. Claire said skin-to-skin tactile stimulation is important for Talia. Important for *her*? To be able to breathe in her sweet, innocent, newborn scent is absolute heaven for *me*! Tears of joy, sadness, fear, and ultimate peace slowly creep down my face, as I gently stroke her soft, peach-fuzz skin, and hum lullabies in her ear. I feel as if someone has given me an incredible drug. The sense of peace and love for her is overwhelming. It is hard to fathom that there is something wrong with her. I see *total* beauty, even with her eyes puffy and her body limp. Why was I afraid to get close before? My heart begins to melt.

The miracle of love…it can melt fear from even the most hurting hearts.

When Rich arrived at the hospital after work today, I encouraged him to hold Talia like this, so he can feel what I felt. Maybe I was a little strong on the encouragement, because he vehemently said he wasn't ready to try it yet. Although I am extremely frustrated with him at first, I want to be empathetic. I know he's just as scared as I was; it's just harder for him to express his feelings. Instead of forcing the issue or making him feel guilty about it, which I normally would have done, I silently pray that God will reach him, so he can find the strength. My heart tells me he'll be ready in due time. I just pray that it will be soon.

> *Until people are ready to face an issue, they will carry protective armor around. They decide when they no longer need it. When trying to coerce another, words fall on deaf ears…prayer falls on My ears.*

Five

Day 9

July 1

I feel more connected to Talia this morning after yesterday's visit. More blood tests come back negative, which means that none of this makes any sense yet. No change for the better; no change for the worse.

My parents came in today. I imagine it must be hard for them to see their daughter in this state of chaos. As we give them an update on Talia's uncertain condition, my mother wipes away tears. I notice the moistness in my father's eyes. My heart aches for both of them. As much as they want to shield us from our pain, I also want to protect them from hurting. I know that I can't. My father has always been a pillar of strength. In fact, I can remember only once that I've seen him cry — when his father died. Now, watching him stand by Talia's side, I sense that perhaps there are many unshed tears that have built up within him through the years. Why does he feel that he has to be so strong?

Because many feel that tears signal weakness, which is far from the truth. Tears are a vehicle to cleanse the soul. And do not try to shield one from pain…to do so would be to shield them from an opportunity to heal.

"Sandy, don't worry honey, she's going to be just fine. I bet they're doing all this testing just to get more money from the insurance companies," my father says.

Although we've always been a look-on-the-bright-side family, this comment sounds utterly ridiculous. In the past, I would have judged him for that cynical comment. But right now I understand that perhaps it is simply my father's way of not wanting to admit that there could really be something wrong with Talia. And I love him for it. It is becoming a little easier for me to understand people's actions without the normal judgments I usually place on them.

> *Love…the greatest healer. The shift in your awareness from judgment to understanding is a lesson that many need to learn in this lifetime. You will help them.*

My parents, as well as all my sisters, are crucial to our survival each day. It takes nearly every ounce of energy to be at the hospital for Talia, so there is very little left over for Ariana. My family has taken turns caring for Ari every day. I feel great comfort knowing that she has loving care in our absence. When we return to my parents' house at the end of the day, weary and tear-strained, we just about collapse on their sofa and give them an update. My mother always has a hot meal waiting for us, as well as one to take home. It is such a blessing to live so close to my family (we all live within 35 minutes of each other). Emotionally, they are my source of strength, and I am grateful for them all.

> *Counting your blessings will always give you sudden bursts of strength to lean on.*

Day 10

July 2

Today I feel as though my prayers are being heard. The nurses noticed that when Talia was "kangaroo-ing" with me this afternoon, she moved more spontaneously and had more independent respiratory activity than she's had up until this point. She responds to me — this is incredible news! I *know* I can make her better! And another miracle happens today. Rich has decided to try the "kangaroo" hold with Talia, so he can feel closer to her. He has her on his chest right now. As I watch the two of them bond during these precious moments, my inner wisdom tells me that the walls around his heart are melting. The picture of this brokenhearted father, snuggling his infant daughter with tears in his eyes, is priceless. I am so proud of him for allowing himself to be vulnerable. Maybe it was the best thing to back off so Rich could decide when he was ready. I realize I have never loved him more. Thank you, God. Maybe you are still watching over us after all.

Always have been, always will be…

Six

Day 11

July 3

Rich's brother, Eddy, and his wife and kids are here from Connecticut to visit and they've brought some cute outfits for Talia. I feel bad that the kids can't see Talia because only adults are allowed in the NICU. It is probably better that way. I don't know if I could have stayed strong in front of them, though no one tells me I have to. I am happy they are here to support Rich.

Talia's doctors still don't know her prognosis. She exhibits the ability to occasionally breathe without any help from the respirator, so they lower her respirator settings to see how well she can do. At one point, she gave us a scare when her face momentarily turned dusky again from not breathing deeply enough.

She has been seizure-free now for a couple of days, most likely from being so heavily sedated. The goal is slowly to decrease her Phenobarbital level while maintaining control over her seizures. I've always liked the challenge of goals, and know that we'll reach this one together. We just have to.

Or else…?

Day 12

The nurses told me that before I arrived here this morning, my sister Susie had already been here very early. She had come in just to hold Talia's hand and quietly sing to her. Susie, who has a great voice, always loved to sing, as did all my sisters. In fact, when we were younger, we sang together and played the guitar at holidays and at church a few times. We sounded pretty good, in three-or four-part harmony. Susie had always been known for singing the loudest. In the summer time, when all the windows were open, you could hear her singing from a couple of houses away! Quite often she'd come right up to us and sing loudly in our ears. She thought it was funny; we thought it hurt. How I wish now that she could do that to Talia. Perhaps it could stir her awake from this deep, dark sleep.

Rich and I meet with the nurse practitioner, Wilma, and ask many questions that come flowing to us about Talia's development. When will she be able to breathe and eat on her own and when the heck will we be able to bring her home so we can all start our normal life together? Wilma advises us that although they don't have answers for us, the team is concerned for Talia. Well, so are we, but I refuse to give up hope. As crazy as it sounds, I know that somehow, some way, she'll be okay, and so will we.

*Are you now realizing that perhaps it was **you** who had to wake up? Many live their lives in a "deep, dark sleep" before they are "awakened" by a crisis in life. Most would rather stay asleep, because it is less painful. Good morning to you, Sandy, this **is** your wake-up call.*

Day 13

What a wonderful morning! Claire asked if I wanted to help give Talia a sponge bath. I was petrified at first because Talia seems so fragile. It was an incredible experience. In moments like these, I imagine that Talia is like any normal baby, precious and adorable. Her curly, dark brown hair smells clean and fresh. We dress her in the cute little, green dress that Claire brought in for her. I want so badly to freeze these moments.

"Real moments" that are noticed and appreciated can last for a lifetime...collect them while you can.

This is also the day to start weaning Talia from the seizure medication to see what level she can tolerate with no seizure activity. She has also been off the respirator since last night and is independently breathing fairly well. So far, so good. Talia's ability to breathe on her own is such a critical marker to us. A thought keeps flashing in my mind. One's ability to breathe is a fundamental necessity of existence, something so elementary, yet I've never been thankful for it! Suddenly my mind is flooded with the innumerable blessings that I, for too long, have taken for granted. Silently, I pray, "God, I'm so sorry that I haven't always fully appreciated all that you've provided. Thank you for all your blessings, large and small, and help me to be continually aware of them." Where these words of gratitude come from, I have not a clue, but they feel good.

A prayer of thankfulness in a time of crisis...that's faith.

Day 14

We got a call from the hospital at 6:00AM. Talia had to be put back on the respirator last night because her breathing was grossly erratic. Whatever high we were on yesterday was stripped away from us with this one phone call. This is beginning to feel like a roller coaster ride that is careening out of control! I read somewhere long ago that we should pray not for our burdens to be lessened, but for stronger shoulders. My shoulders are about knee level at this point, and I'm not sure how much more I can handle emotionally.

With My strength, you can (and will) handle it all.

This afternoon, Rich and I had a family meeting with the entire staff of doctors, nurses, and the social worker assigned to Talia's case. They are as frustrated as we are, not knowing what is wrong with our baby. They mention that her symptoms resemble "Ohtahara's syndrome.' That means she has "infantile spasms," along with a "characteristically abnormal EEG pattern." So, basically, nothing is new.

Since she is still seizure-free, they set two immediate goals for Talia. First they would like to see her be able to breathe without the respirator, and secondly they want to try and feed her orally, rather than through the nasal tube. They'll see how she manages, then reevaluate her prognosis. The phrase "it's getting worrisome" is spoken more than once during that meeting. Those words don't quite register. Perhaps I am blocking out what they are trying to tell me. I want to stay focused on the positives here and now and not look too far into the future.

After the meeting, I am able to spend quiet moments alone with Talia. She sleeps so peacefully, and looks so innocent. She has no idea that her condition is causing such anguish to the people who love her. I whisper into her tiny ear, "My sweet, little angel, why is this happening to us?" Though I don't fully understand it, I am beginning to sense that there must be answers hiding somewhere in the midst of this heartache and confusion. I've come to believe that every event in life has a purpose. Still, I am having a difficult time seeing the purpose here.

> *Sometimes life doesn't seem to make sense at all, especially when the darkness of the unknown lurks right in front of your eyes. And sometimes, the only **sense** there is comes in the form of the healing and growth you choose to experience.*

Day 15

July 7

Talia is unusually active today, fortunately not with seizures. Her grasp is definitely present and she has had her eyes open for about an hour. She's done that a couple of times before but only for a few moments. In the past she has just stared with a fixed gaze, but today, it looks as if she's able to follow an object for a couple of seconds. The nurses also think that she seems a little more responsive to sound. Part of me is scared to get my hopes up again, but with all these positive signs, I just know Talia is going to prove the medical community wrong. I am convinced she is going to be a normal child — all it takes is believing! In fact, I believe it so strongly that I can actually visualize myself on "Oprah," telling the story of our "miracle baby"! I refuse to give up hope.

This afternoon, however, Talia had another MRI and started seizing right in the middle of the procedure. When the nurses told me, it was as if someone took a knife to my heart, tapping it ever so slowly inducing a slow, painful stream of fear. So much for the visualization.

My hopes and dreams are now shattered. This is too much for me to handle. I feel like a battle-weary soldier, with his head hung low, ready to surrender. God, please give me strength. How will I ever make it through this in one piece?

In your own words, "All it takes is believing." Surrender, and you will find peace that will keep you "in one piece."

Seven

Day 16

July 8

Our morning ritual, even before we get out of bed is to call the hospital to check on Talia's status. This morning, the nurse told us that they extubated Talia once again, and she was doing well. They were beginning to wonder if she might have some physical abnormality that obstructs her airway. It would explain her not being able to breathe effectively. So, when they extubated her last night, they supported her neck to help keep her airway open. Anything to help her, but I am having a hard time getting overly optimistic.

We brought Ariana with us to the hospital today. Ari loves seeing that her little gray dinosaur is keeping close watch over her baby sister. I wonder what must go through Ariana's mind, seeing Talia surrounded by all the elaborate monitors and other equipment. Is she as scared as we are? If she is, she hides it pretty well. Ari is so cute with Talia, rubbing her arm, whispering softly to her, "Hi, Talia, it's me, Ari. Hi honey." She is so gentle with her. My mind wanders as I observe this loving bond between two sisters. Will they ever be able to run around outside together, play with dolls, fight over clothes, walk hand in hand? If I let my mind drift into the future, overwhelming sadness takes over, so I stay in the present moment and savor it.

Day 17

Our early morning call brought unwanted news. The doctor to whom we spoke was new to Talia's care. We had never heard his name before. He nonchalantly conveyed that they re-intubated Talia again last night because her breathing was highly abnormal. At one point her skin turned bluish/gray. I felt as though the wind was knocked out of me. It took all my strength to refrain from screaming into the phone, "No, don't tell me this. I don't want to hear it!" I processed nothing more from that point on.

The doctor continued, though, with no emotion in his voice, "You may need to consider a tracheotomy as a long-term option, since Talia has had such a poor time keeping her airway open on her own."

Tracheotomy??? Where was all this coming from? Who was this man delivering this blunt news? I instantly decided I didn't like him one bit.

A common initial reaction when one hears the truth.

Rich and I came to the hospital much earlier today. We sat in the hospital parking lot, bracing ourselves for yet another day of uncertainty. I asked Rich if he would pray with me, something we've never, ever done before. I felt the need to pray, and believed that if Rich and I combined our prayers together, perhaps they'd somehow carry more strength. We sat there holding hands. At first, neither one of us knew what to say. This awkwardness soon left.

"God, please help our little Talia, help her to get well, " I began.

Rich added, "Give us some answers and the strength and understanding to handle them."

Together, we whispered, "Amen."

Though it was a short prayer, it was spoken from our hearts, which have been beaten by a painful blow. In the quiet, cramped quarters of his car, Rich embraced me. We both immediately had a sense of inner peace that was not there a few moments earlier.

Why have we never prayed together before? He was raised Jewish, but is not at all close to his faith. Since we don't usually talk to each other about God, I guess I was hesitant to ask him, not knowing how he'd respond. After this prayer, we knew that together we'll be able to handle anything.

Prayer always leads to peace, especially when you leave your hurts in My hands.

At Talia's bedside, our frustration mounts when the doctors have nothing new to tell us during their rounds. We need to know more. We need answers. And we are ready to ask some questions we haven't dared ask before. We request a family conference with Dr. Stewart, Talia's primary doctor, Wilma, and Mary, her nurse practitioners, and Cindy, her respiratory therapist.

A few hours later, as soon as all the players were available, we assembled in Wilma's tiny office. Rich and I sat close to each other on the sofa for support, each of us silently repeating our prayers.

When you ask, prepare to receive...

We needed to know everything. So we started asking. "What are the possible and probable outcomes for Talia? What are the chances of her ever being a normal little girl? Will she ever be aware of her surroundings? What would be the worst-case scenario?" I hated even saying those words aloud. Part of me wanted to hold my ears, so I wouldn't hear the reply. However, my soul knew it was time to hear more. Time stood still during that next hour. Their mouths moved, but each word seemed to be spoken in slow motion. Dr. Stewart was compassionate, but her answers came with crushing blows.

Only a portion of what she said registered, "...still no definite cause of Talia's status...no definitive prognosis...HOWEVER, poor outcomes of her three EEG's...prognosis is grim...IF she survives past the next month...will likely die within early infancy...if she didn't die *then*...and even *if* she could ever breathe on her own...SHE WILL MOST LIKELY NEVER BE ABLE TO WALK...SEE...HEAR...TALK...SMILE...LAUGH...COMMUNICATE..."

I tried to stop listening, because the words stung too much. Regardless of what was said, what I processed was "...your daughter is going to die." My deepest fears were confirmed. The knife that was tapping on my heart now pierced its way through to the other side. Wracked with pain, Rich and I sobbed in each other's arms.

We were left alone to process our intense emotions in private. I told Rich that I am so proud that he didn't feel that he had to be strong in front of the nurses. Was he at last allowing himself to be fully vulnerable by feeling the pain? Perhaps he was scaling the walls around his heart that he had built, when he believed that love hurts. Faraway, I heard the sound of my *own* protective walls crumble as well — there was no use for them anymore.

Truth and love, when combined, can melt even the most
frozen, isolated parts of your heart...then can you heal.

Wilma returned a short while later to check on us.

"Are you regretful of all the information you heard," she asked. "Was it too much at one time?"

"Not really," I responded. "Up until this point, however, I only wanted to hear the positives, holding on to any remote morsels of hope. But we reached the point where we needed to face the truth."

Although I was grateful for their honesty, I sensed it was going to be difficult to imagine any positive outcomes, to see any hope. Wilma came over to us and hugged both of us tightly. Could she even understand our pain? It must be especially hard for her, since she is seven months pregnant with her first child. I can only imagine the fears that must go through her mind as she works with all of these critical newborns.

I also wondered how all the doctors and nurses stay so strong, while parents like us, who had sick children, fell apart emotionally all around them. How did they not take the pain home with them? They must have learned how to walk a fine line of empathy and emotional detachment. Wilma explained that they have counselors to talk to in situations like these, because at times they aren't so strong emotionally either. Thank you God, for the staff here at Beth Israel. They truly play an integral part of our healing process day after day. God bless them all.

And you are an integral part of their healing process, too.
You are all connected.

After our fateful meeting, we returned to Talia, barely able to see her through our puffy, reddened eyes. It is as if everything has shifted. Looking at her now, she appears even more angelic, sleeping quite peacefully. With the nurse's help, I gently cradle Talia in my arms. My pain grows more intense, now knowing far more than I had before. She doesn't look like she is going to die.

I think about the irony of our combined prayer earlier this morning, and how much peace it brought us. What happened to that peace? My mind is filled only with the unbelievable reality that Talia may die. Anger is dancing with my fear.

Have we done something wrong to deserve this, God? What about our prayers? Why aren't they being answered? In an instant, from a place deep within me, I hear...

> *Sandy, you asked for strength and understanding, and you are beginning to sense My messages for you in your soul. You'll soon realize that Talia is already "perfect" as she is. Listen to your heart and soul, for that is how you'll hear My words for you.*

Tears still stream down my cheeks as I whisper into her ear, "My innocent, sweet, little Talia. I love you so much. I'm so sad to think that you won't have the chance to ride on a pony, or build sand castles, or eat ice cream. And I'll never be able to wipe away your tears. I'll never watch you in a dance recital. I'll never help you get ready for your senior prom. I'll never hear the words a mother longs to hear from her child — 'I love you, Mommy.' " Oh God, why is this happening? When are we all going to wake up from this nightmare?

Almost immediately, the answer gently came to my thoughts...

> *Perhaps this **was** Talia's dream...to reawaken your soul...to help you and Rich learn to "feel" once again...to help you shift your awareness in life. You can wake up whenever you're ready. This "nightmare" is labeled as such by your terms, and when you're at a certain point in your journey, you'll realize how much growth came from this pain.*

We desperately needed to go home and see Ariana. Her playfulness and vitality give us energy when we have none left. We need life breathed back into us, and Ariana has an abundance of it for all of us. On the car ride home, I silently thanked God for having blessed us with Ariana.

It has struck me lately that often in the deep throes of sadness, thoughts of gratitude, love, compassion, or understanding come to me from out of nowhere. I'm not quite sure how that can be, but I welcome these fleeting moments, since they bring peace into my confused state of mind. As we approached home, I silently wondered how in the world parents begin to process the fact that their child is going to die. Apparently, we were going to find out.

Eight

Day 18

July 10

We are informed today that the chief of neurology from Children's Hospital, Dr. Volpe, has been consulted about Talia's case. At some point, we will meet with him to get his opinion of her status. We are still trying to grasp at any straw that may be left.

One of our last straws is a procedure called a bronchoscopy that will be performed tomorrow. During this delicate procedure, the specialist from Children's will insert a tiny camera down Talia's throat and ascertain whether or not there is a structural reason that she can't keep her airway open and breathe on her own. If there is a physical obstruction, they'll obviously just operate and remove whatever is causing the problem. Then she'll be able to breathe normally, and we can all go home and be a family. Seems simple enough to me. Their sense, however, is that it is not a physical obstruction. They feel it is more likely a neurological disorder that holds a more severe outcome. Please, God, let there be an obstruction.

Day 19

Well, this was Talia's big day. They transported her by ambulance to Children's Hospital in Boston for the bronchoscopy. Although we didn't get to be with her during the ride, her nurses sent along her little, gray dinosaur in the ambulance for protection and comfort. They are so thoughtful.

After obtaining all the necessary signatures, they transferred Talia to the operating room for what would be a few hours. Rich and I anxiously waited in the pediatric ward, pacing back and forth, closely holding each other for strength, half-watching those daytime talk shows on the most ludicrous subjects. "Doesn't anyone know what we are dealing with? Doesn't anyone care?" I wanted to scream. Just then, we saw a young boy, probably about ten years old, being wheeled by on a gurney. His enlarged head must have been swollen to four times its normal size. It was shocking. What quickly struck me was that, while we've had to endure this intense pain for 19 days, some parents endure it for years. I suddenly felt the need to thank God for sparing us from prolonged pain.

Later in the morning, we ventured down to the cafeteria, trying to pass some time. There, we saw a young man around 20 years old sitting with an older gentleman, whom I imagined was his father. This boy had profound facial abnormalities, and my first reaction was one of repulsion. I was scared by the sight of his face, and wanted to turn quickly away and pity him. I wondered how many people who had crossed his path before had run from the sight of him? Instantaneously, my thoughts were transformed by a whisper from within.

True beauty lies within. Do not judge others based on their appearance.

I felt ashamed, thinking about how many people I have judged in the past, based on appearance. Suddenly, my heart was filled with compassion for this young man. I wanted to walk over and tell him that he had touched my life. I wanted to tell him that I felt love for him, but I didn't. I sat in my chair and prayed that this boy's life be continually blessed. God was surely using him to help teach compassion, if people were ready to learn. Thank you, God for sending us to Children's Hospital to open my eyes a little more to Your grace and beauty and love for all of us.

I didn't understand how it was possible that I was seeing things from a different point of view. I was beginning to hear the whispers of my soul and was talking to God as if he was a personal friend and confidante. Oh, no. Have I turned into one of those religious freaks that I had judged so harshly way back when? I didn't really think so.

You are not a "freak;" your eyes have seen the glory.

In the afternoon, Talia's doctor approached us with the results from her procedure. I was unable to read her face as she walked over to us. "Please let there be an obstruction," I prayed as the doctor moved closer. She looked somber as she finally reached us and looked squarely into our eyes. "We found no obstruction."

The realization slowly hit that we had nothing left to hold on to. This procedure held the last card that we were waiting to turn over. We'd been dealt the card of death.

Please remember that even in your darkest moments, you are never, ever alone.

Shortly thereafter, Dr. Volpe met with us to discuss his assessment of Talia's case.

He explained that her chances of being even slightly normal were grim. "In similar, rare cases I've seen, the child has died in the newborn to early infancy stage, or has faced severe mental retardation. Talia's case is far worse."

As we listened to this small, wise man, there was no outpouring of emotion from either Rich or me. It was as if this doctor merely confirmed something we already knew. It was no longer IF she was going to die but WHEN. We know we must brace ourselves for the long road ahead that seems to have no happy ending.

Talia spent the night at Children's Hospital. There was a little girl about Ariana's age in a nearby crib. I didn't know why she was here, but her eyes reflected the same sadness we felt in our hearts. Although the staff at Children's was wonderful, everything seemed darker and colder to us. We longed for the comfort of our familiar surroundings at Beth Israel. We missed the smiles of her nurses and her special little corner in the NICU. We decided that if Talia was going to die soon, we would feel better if she could be back at Beth Israel.

Day 20

July 12

Our wishes were granted. She was transferred back here to Beth Israel this morning — gray dinosaur in tow. Being back at Beth Israel feels like we're home. We have established a strong bond with the staff here in just three short weeks. Since yesterday's development, our visits with Talia begin to take on a different tone. While tears still flow freely, I am slowly accepting the truth. I have no choice but to come to terms with the fact that Talia is going to die. I'm learning a new lesson. When in pain, it does no good to bang your head continually against the wall, ignoring the truth, and trying to force your preferred outcome to manifest itself. I am beginning to first accept our reality, and I know I'll need to come to some sort of peace with it. I ask the nurses about other families they know whose babies have died. Do they survive the pain? Is there love and laughter again? I think I already know the answers, but sense it must be a long journey back to one's heart after a deep loss.

The journey back to one's heart is usually paved with pain, fear, tears, and more pain. When it gets that painful, too many turn to destructive habits to dull the pain. If they would only continue along the journey to growth that follows — surrender...awakening to a higher power... understanding...compassion...peace...love...life!

Another family meeting with Talia's team of doctors was held today to discuss what the course of treatment will be. The options are fairly limited. They can perform a tracheotomy to create an airway and a gastrostomy to feed her through her stomach, which will sustain her life. This means she would be respirator-dependent indefinitely. From the team's previous knowledge and experience, her life would probably be extended briefly. However, "she would suffer continual, intractable seizures and severe mental/neurological retardation and would likely die within her first year." In essence, it would be a short-term fix, simply prolonging the inevitable.

The other option is to redirect her care. This means they would take her off the respirator, provide comfort measures only, and allow nature to take its course. Either way, they are sure Talia is going to eventually die. The first choice would buy us some time. Time for what, I'm not sure, because there is no way to escape from the pain of her impending death. Although the latter choice would be the tougher one to make, it would allow us to start grieving sooner, with the hope of moving forward with our lives, although that seems unimaginable. Do we have the courage to take her off the respirator, knowing that she would soon die? Would we be giving up too soon? What if she makes a miraculous turnaround? And who are we to play God? I pray for wisdom to help us make the right decision. Somehow, I know that we will.

> *There are no right or wrong decisions...only ones that you or others judge to be right or wrong. Whatever decision you make will be the right one for you — for there will be lessons on every path.*

Privately, Rich and I discuss the options. We easily agree on what we feel is best for Talia.

Later in the afternoon, at another family meeting, we informed them of our decision to allow nature to take its course. We also talked about our longing to have Talia be an organ donor when she dies. If we can help other individuals through what we are experiencing, it will give more meaning to Talia's life. It will help her memories live on. Perhaps it will make some sense of this crushing experience.

> *It matters not what you experience in life. The key is to use your experiences to help others heal.*

In order to take her off life support, the hospital needs a written evaluation from Dr. Volpe and a recommendation from a neonatologist not currently involved in her care. The paperwork can take a couple of days. Although our decision was made with love in our hearts, the phrase "take her off life support" sounds so harsh, so mean, so final. It means that we are going to let our little baby die. It is unfathomable to think about letting her go.

> *Sometimes the hardest decisions, made with the utmost love in your heart, involve letting go.*

Nine

Day 21

July 13

There are two small, intimate rooms in the main hallway of the NICU. We pass by these rooms countless times on our way to visit Talia. The doors to these rooms are always open, and the curtains are always pulled back. The rooms have always been empty, and I never understood the purpose for them. Talia is moved into one of these private rooms today and I now know that they are for babies who are not going to live. The room is not to keep them in isolation, but to offer families a chance to spend quality time with their baby before he or she dies. I have a sick feeling in the pit of my stomach when I learn this, because reality is sinking in. After a while though, I am grateful to be here in this room. It feels warmer and more cozy, if that is at all possible, given the circumstances.

They waive any rules about visiting hours and how many visitors she can have at one time. Anyone can come in now to see our beloved angel. Will anyone *want* to come and see her, knowing she is going to die? Will it be too hard for them to bear? Will it be too hard for *us* to bear?

Shortly after Talia was born, I had called Reverend Paul, the minister at Central Square Congregational Church (the same church I'd been attending off and on since that Christmas Eve long ago) to ask for prayers for Talia. Reverend Paul is a wonderful, sweet man with salt and pepper hair. He has a kind demeanor, and it was always easy to talk to him. He came to the hospital once already to visit with us and with Talia. When we realized the severity of her condition, I called him again to set a date for Talia's baptism. Not having had a formal religious education, I wasn't sure what baptism was all about. Reverend Paul explained, in a nutshell, that after Talia died, she'd spend eternal life with God.

It is ironic that this was the day we had chosen for Talia's baptism, having just made the formidable decision to take her off of life support. The baptism service was performed right in Talia's room. Rich and I cried as Reverend Paul gently blessed Talia with words that seemed to encircle her with love. Talia has never looked more peaceful.

When we got home at night, I called Rich's mother in Connecticut to give her an update. I explained what had transpired since we last spoke.

"Mom, the bronchoscopy found nothing. There's not much else they can do for her, other than keep her comfortable. No one knows when, but Talia is going to die."

"Oh, I'm so sorry."

"I know you were waiting until she came home before you came to see her, but it doesn't look like that's going to happen. Maybe you'd like to come and see her in the hospital before she...dies?" It was hard to get the words out.

"Oh, honey, I want to, but...I don't know...I'm afraid it would be...too difficult."

I heard the fear in her voice. My first reaction was disappointment that she would never know her granddaughter. Gulping in my feelings, I hung up the phone. Almost immediately,

I understood that her heart had been through many losses. Both of her parents died when she was in her late teens and she lost her husband a few years ago. Perhaps visiting Talia would reopen deep wounds. I was starting to realize that we can heal if we allow ourselves to face the pain and not run from it. I wonder if she was choosing to turn away from pain, hoping it would be easier to deal with that way. Although I empathized with her, my heart ached for Rich. He was proud of Talia, and he wanted to show her off to the world.

Day 21

July 13

Talia met the first of many of her cousins today. Susie is here with her two kids, Rico and Roxanne, and they have brought Ariana too. I try to explain to the kids that Talia is going to die, that she is very sick, and is going to be with God in heaven. Ariana replies, "Oh, when will she come back home?" How on earth do I explain this to a two-and-one-half year old when I don't even fully comprehend it myself? Rico, who is five, is much more inquisitive. As he holds Talia, he asks so many adorable questions, like, "How is she going to get to heaven? What will she eat in heaven? Will she be an angel? How will she get her wings?" I love that kids are able to say what is on their minds, so openly and honestly. I wish I had the answers for him. I wish I had the answers for me.

You do, dear child, look within…for the answers, for the strength, for the lessons.

Many times I feel as though I am observing this chapter of my life from a point of view outside of my own, from a more evolved, wiser perspective. Whenever this happens, I sense that there are lessons we will be learning and that we will grow and heal. And in these moments, a profound sense of peace sweeps through my body. It happens to me again today, watching the kids take turns holding Talia. Sadness tugs at my heart, knowing that Talia will be with us only for a short time, and that she won't grow older with the rest of her cousins. However, during this intensely painful time, a sense of comfort comes to me from out of nowhere, reminding me that Talia will soon be at peace and will be with God forever. What is this shift that is occurring within me? How is it possible to experience two extreme emotions at the same time?

> *You've cried out for help; you've opened your heart; now you can expect the pain to ease. It's called the grace of God, available to all who are choosing to receive it.*

Ten

Day 22

July 14

At home last night, at around 8:00pm, we got a phone call from Rich's sister, Eileen. She and Rich's mother had driven up from Connecticut and were calling us from Talia's room. It was a surprise to both of us, and we were thrilled! What was happening here? Perhaps his mother was already on her own healing journey back to her heart. We invited them to come to our house afterwards to visit and spend the night.

When they arrived at our house, the air was a little tense as I rambled on and on. "Isn't Talia adorable? Was she still wearing that pink headband? Did she open her eyes for you at all?" All I wanted to do was talk about Talia, but I sensed it made Rich's mother very uncomfortable, because she kept changing the subject. It hurt, but I knew I had to respect where she is on her healing journey. So I took a deep breath, held in my sadness, made some excuse about being tired, and went upstairs to the bedroom.

> *Sandy, don't try to force others to feel what you feel. You must be concerned only with your own healing path at this time. It is up to others to decide if and when they are going to choose to heal themselves.*

Today we still wait for the two assessments so they can take Talia off life support. A doctor informs us that she cannot be an organ donor. It has something to do with the fact that they have no clear diagnosis but believe it to be metabolic in nature, and that she will not be "brain dead" before she dies. This is one more disappointing blow to our hearts. We are trying to put the jumbled pieces of this puzzle together and feel the need to make a difference somehow, somewhere. We so badly need to find some meaning to this whole emotional experience. I am beginning to understand that there is a purpose in all of this, but I'm not quite sure what it is. I truly don't think God would ever play a joke like this on anyone. If we can just help others through what we're experiencing...

There are no "cruel jokes," only opportunities for spiritual growth. Patience, my dear child...your experience with Talia will help many, many people. More so than you could ever imagine. Let go and let the process unfold on its own timing.

The social worker assigned to us came by today. We've spoken with her before. I didn't care for her at first because she always seemed to look at us with pity. But today, she doesn't have that look on her face. She is like a dear friend who has a strong shoulder on which we need to lean.

How wonderful it is that one's perception of another can change when one's heart is open to them.

She asks me how my family typically handled grief. I explained that, in my eyes, my parents are strong individuals, who do not dwell on sadness or pain, but find the will to survive through it. Since I saw strength as a positive trait, perhaps I had always thought that giving in to sadness signaled weakness. I was only five when my mother lost her father to cancer. Then, less than one year later, her twenty-nine-year-old brother, who had three very young children, died in a tragic car accident on Easter morning. My mother told me recently that her faith in God carried her through that excruciatingly painful period. I also remember my grandmother, Sattymommy, crying a lot because she desperately missed her husband and son through the long years after they died. Whenever she'd start to cry, she'd always apologize, as if she were ashamed of her sadness. I am thankful that I've chosen not to carry on that trait. I see it differently now. If I had to hold in all my sadness in order to be strong, I think I would've exploded by now.

> *Emotions are there to be expressed, otherwise they can block the path to one's heart.*

I spoke at length with this social worker about all the potential visitors coming in to see Talia. I explained that, although I would love to have relatives and friends continue to visit, I understand if they feel too uncomfortable, especially knowing that Talia is going to die. I guess I want to spare everyone from excessive pain. She comments that people may be sorry later if they don't spend time with Talia. I don't want anyone to have regrets. I'm just trying once again to shield others from hurting. As painful as this is, it is still easier for me to be in pain than to see someone else suffering. I've always said to Rich that I'm glad I had to go through childbirth, because I couldn't bear to see him in that much pain! He'd always joked back that he couldn't bear to see himself in that much pain either! For as long as I can remember, whenever someone I cared about faced any kind of challenge, my tendency was to quickly jump in and fix them, so they could be happy again. One lesson I'm learning through all of this is that it's okay to feel emotions other than happiness, and that people have to choose to help themselves when it comes to healing. I can't do it for them.

> *Good, Sandy, you're catching on…to shield anyone from pain is to shield them from an opportunity to heal, and an opportunity to grow. There is a lesson here for you. You don't have to fix anyone. Allow them to be, and love and accept them **as they are**. If they so choose, they will heal.*

Later tonight, Dr. Volpe stopped by with his final assessment.

"Because Talia's latest EEG showed the same disturbing pattern," he said calmly, "her prognosis is extremely unfavorable, with no chance for a normal outcome and a high likelihood of death or severe neurological consequences, *if* she survives the newborn period."

As he spoke, each word seemed to cut through a new layer of my heart. Even though we had prepared ourselves for this, it seems more final now. His report supports our decision to take Talia off the ventilator, allowing her to die in peace.

After he left, Rich and I held Talia. Although we earlier felt a certain degree of comfort in our decision, we are now scared to death! Or perhaps it is scared *of* death. What if we are making the wrong decision? What if we can't handle it? What if we never recover? What if Talia dies right in front of us? There are so many "what ifs."

> *Your "what ifs" are not reality. They are merely "fear" trying to hold you back from living in the moment. Stay present in the moment at hand, and you shall find the courage to move on.*

Thank God, Claire was here when Dr. Volpe left. We are blessed with the best of nurses, but there is something so special about Claire. She is gentle and understanding, and seems especially connected with us and with Talia. Tonight, we allow ourselves to voice many of our fearful questions about what to expect in the next few days. I don't know how much I can handle.

I asked nervously, "Claire, how will we know if Talia is near death? What will she look like when she...dies?"

Claire was straightforward, yet gentle in her answers. "After they extubate Talia, she may breathe for a while. We'll make sure she isn't in any pain, but at some point, her breathing may become more labored, and she may look like she's gasping for breath." As soon as she says this, I feel myself trying to catch my own breath.

Claire continued calmly. "As it becomes more and more difficult for her, she may start to lose color and may turn dusky or bluish as she nears death. No one knows how long this process will take — it could be hours or days — no one can be sure. Some parents choose to set up a cot in their child's room to be there and hold their baby as it dies. Some choose to give their baby a bath after it has died. It's up to you. You need to do whatever you decide is right for you."

You've got to be kidding me. Hold a dead baby? Give it a bath afterwards? How gross. This entire morbid discussion gives me the creeps.

Do not judge that which you have not yet experienced.

Eleven

Day 23

My mind is still whirling from our discussion with Claire last night. I can't allow myself to think too far into the future. I need all the strength I have to stay present in the moment.

The care team has called for a meeting in the conference room because the letter from the second neonatologist arrived today. In the meeting, the letter was read to us. It gave us a little more comfort in our decision. Here is what it said:

"I have been asked to provide an outside opinion on the parents' request to redirect care away from intensive medical therapy towards comfort measures only. I have not previously treated Talia, but have been aware of her plight for the past three weeks. I have reviewed her medical records and clinical course. I have spoken with the medical, NNP and nursing team, as well as with the consultant, and have examined the infant.

I construe my role as threefold. First, I must ensure that the evaluation has been thorough. Second, I must ensure that the decision-making process has been open and fair. Third, I must be sure that the result is within the scope of ethical practice for our NICU.

The central issue is that Talia has severe to profound dysfunction of the Central Nervous System, resulting in seizures that were exceedingly difficult to control, as well as persistent central hypo ventilation and/or apnea. The cause of the severe brain damage remains obscure, despite a comprehensive medical evaluation. The medical team has performed a battery of metabolic, toxicological and hormonal tests, obtained repeated scans of the brain, and followed serial neurologic exams and EEGs. The lack of a diagnosis makes it more difficult to offer a prognosis with great certainty, and seriously complicates the deliberations in this case.

Nonetheless, there is much that we can prognosticate from what we know. While some recovery is not impossible (since we do not know the cause), extensive and irremediable damage has already occurred. The devastating implications of the central apnea and burst suppression pattern on EEG mean that normal survival is foreclosed. Although it is not possible to specify the level of future developmental deficits, it seems highly unlikely that they will be only moderate, but much more likely to be severe to profound. Her life span will surely be foreshortened.

The decision-making revolves around continuing to provide intensive care (mechanical ventilation) via tracheotomy in order to sustain the infant's chances for such a limited survival. The care team has deliberated in a fair and open process, seeking consultation from appropriate specialists, engaging the parents, and not rushing to judgment. The parents' understanding and emotions have evolved over the past three weeks. It is clear from the staff and the notes that they are caring and committed to the child's welfare.

It seems rational to me that a child in such a position could reasonably ask to forego life-support since it does not offer a chance of cure, is painful and invasive, and may only prolong the infant's life in such a compromised state. The parents request to redirect care is a reflection of their balancing the costs of daily pain and suffering against the real but limited quality of existence. This would seem entirely consistent with what the infant might request. I conclude that this is clearly an area where the benefits of further treatment are ambiguous at best, and patient (parental) autonomy should be respected. Please let them help her."

Phrases like, "...child in such a position could reasonably ask to forego life-support..." and "...what the infant might request..." haunted me. All this time, we were thinking about what *we* wanted. Would Talia really choose to die? The thought of our little baby choosing to die made me feel incredibly sad. Was it to spare us a lifetime of pain and suffering? What if she wanted to live? How could we ever be sure we were making the right decision?

Oh God, please help us to know that we are making the right decision!

My fear was running rampant but my soul sensed that Talia came here to do her work, and now she wanted to be free.

The plans were to take Talia off the respirator and provide comfort measures only. This meant that no heroic lifesaving procedures would be done. As part of this decision, they presented us with a "Do Not Resuscitate" order for us to sign. Looking at this piece of paper, every morsel of maternal instinct was engaged in battle. "You cannot do this to your child," it seemed to scream at me. "It is your job as a mother to protect your innocent child from harm, from death, and you are sentencing her to death." My heart pounded, my hands shook, and a steady stream of tears fell as I stared at the DNR order. Guilt found its way to my heart, but I tried not to let it make its home there. Still hoping that we were doing what Talia wanted us to do for her, we signed the DNR out of our love for her.

They told us that she would probably live for 12 to 36 hours, based on how poorly she had done in her past attempts at breathing on her own.

God, please be with us now. Give us a sign that we're doing the right thing.

We left the meeting room and came back to Talia's room to see her before they took her off the respirator. She seems very restless, not her usual lethargic self. It seems as if she is trying to tell us something. It actually looks as if she *wants* to be free. Thank you, God, I'm taking this as a sign. My heart feels lighter.

Ask and you shall receive.

Twelve

1:00PM — the countdown began, and my fear was mounting. Would she be able to breathe? Would she start to choke and gasp for air? Rich and I were much too anxious to watch them extubate Talia. We stood outside her room, and held onto one another. Moments later, Talia's nurse called us back in.

I'm amazed at how Talia looks — absolutely beautiful and peaceful. She is breathing very comfortably. They hand her to me to hold, and I feel my breathing become one with hers. I can cuddle her tightly now. It is an incredible experience to be able to hold her freely and walk around without the restricting tubes and beeping monitors! I savor each long moment I have with her. It feels so wonderful, not at all as though I have a baby who is slowly dying.

Because she is still living, and you are living in the moment.

We have brought in some of the outfits that Talia had received as gifts. We chose a little white jumper with tiny pink flowers to put on her. I also dressed her in a matching headband. What a little doll — she is such a beautiful baby! Rich seems to feel more at ease with Talia, too. The chaos that has surrounded us for so long seems to have disappeared momentarily. We are cherishing its absence. It almost feels as if I'm living in a make believe world right now. I even remember laughing with Rich a few times today, bringing lighthearted, healing moments to an emotionally charged day. Although it is hard to describe, in Talia's room today I once again feel an overwhelming sense of being protected, a sense of inner peace like I've never felt before.

How can I ever explain this to anyone? They'll think I'm nuts.

Unless they too have felt My presence, and the presence of angels.

Day 24

July 16

When we arrived home last night, I tried to relax by writing about some of the events that were rocking my life. When I was younger, I spent an extensive amount of time in my bedroom, writing in my diary about the day's events, about my feelings, about nothing at all. In fact, I kept diaries on and off for about 12 years. Since then, I seemed to write only when I was in a crisis and needed to clear my mind. Obviously, this was qualifying as one of those times.

So last night I sat on the couch and quieted my chattering mind with some deep breaths. I sensed that I needed to listen to the wisdom and guidance from within. Pondering the questions, "What do I need to know at this time? What message do I need to hear?" I allowed my ego to take a step back, in order to allow a stream of consciousness to be present. Suddenly my pen seemed to be writing on its own, quickly skimming the page. A few moments later, I was shocked to read what was written on the page.

The belief "there is a reason for all that happens" is valid. The knowledge may not be revealed to you for many months, years, or even longer, but feel that there is a higher order working things through your lives. To have lost a child is devastating, but you must look at the meaning of her life; what she symbolizes. Talia was eager to be born unto you to show you lessons in just these 4 weeks. You have learned quickly, and you will be able to carry these new-found strengths with you forever. And they'll help you to reach new heights of awareness in your life.

Do not look at her death as a sad time, but rejoice in her spirit's presence in your life. So it should be with anyone you encounter in our lives — to love them as much as possible, and learn from them. If you can keep yourselves open to those two tasks in your daily lives, you can find freedom from that which burdens most people. Your lives can be fulfilling to an even greater degree by keeping yourselves open. As difficult as this process has been for both of you, feel blessed that you have been able to experience it. You were chosen because of your ability to learn from it. Remember Talia not for what she could never be, but for how she helped enrich your lives, and the lives around you.

"…born unto you…new heights of awareness…" Whoa! Where was that coming from? I was a little spooked while I read it, because it all sounded pretty profound, and the words didn't sound as though they were from me. I ran upstairs where Rich was watching TV.

"Rich, Rich, I think I just got a written message from God! You have to read what it says!"

He was impressed after he read it, but being practical, he insisted it came from me. "Sandy, as long as it makes you happy, believe what you want," he said sweetly.

Aargh, he has always been so pragmatic. But I didn't care. I knew that this message came *through* me, not *from* me. I'd heard of people who were able to receive divine messages through automatic writing. Whatever it was and wherever it was coming from, it brought incredible insight, wisdom, and inner peace to me. With a smile in my heart, I whispered, "Thank you, God."

> *With a smile in My "heart," I shout to you, You're welcome.*
> *I'm glad you opened your heart enough to receive the*
> *message — you were tough to get through to.*

What a day filled with love and pride for our little angel. My parents came in for a visit, as did my sisters Cindy and Penny, Penny's husband, and all of their children. Talia is the star of the show, "posing" for pictures with everyone, sleeping the entire time. As we capture these keepsake moments to hold onto forever, tears are mixed with smiles. I'm learning not to run away from the tears but to embrace them, for they signal the healing of one's heart. I feel so close to my parents, to my family, to Rich and Ariana. I feel an abundance of love for anyone who comes into this room.

> *Love…the almighty conqueror.*

It has now been over 24 hours since Talia began breathing independently, and she appears normal, like a perfectly healthy newborn, a real live Sleeping Beauty. She's still breathing comfortably, although we have observed a couple of scary moments when she'll start to look pale and dusky. With the very next breath, inevitably a little deeper, her skin once again returns to its usual pretty pink. If that's what she'll look like when she dies, we feel we can handle it. We decide that we absolutely *do* want to be here with her when she dies. We just have to be. But for right now, so far, so good — she is still alive! Do we dare get our hopes up that she continue living? The grim reality that she is dying seems like a faded memory from another lifetime. If only it was.

While I have moments of strength, full of love and hope, in an instant they can be swallowed up by the canyon of fear on whose edge I am constantly teetering. After everyone leaves and Rich and I find ourselves alone in Talia's room, fearful thoughts begin to echo through my mind. I fear that she will die. What if we aren't here with her? I also fear that she will live. Will we have to take her home in this condition, or will she stay here indefinitely? I don't know *what* I am hoping for anymore. The nurse on duty assures me that Talia can stay here as long as we wish. In essence, we don't have to make any more decisions yet. Thank God!

Rich and I have decided to spend the night at the hospital, in response to our fear that she may not make it through to tomorrow. For a change of scenery, we brought Talia to the family room just outside the NICU. It's equipped with a couch, a chair, a TV, and a door for privacy. As the hours slowly tick by, we take turns cuddling with Talia, while the other tries to get some rest. Every time Talia makes the slightest move, we panic, thinking she is having a seizure. Each time she exhales, we hold our breath waiting for her to inhale again. Needless to say, we don't get much sleep, but it doesn't matter. The sand in the hourglass of Talia's life is slowly dwindling.

And when she dies, the "sand" will be replenished forever.

Thirteen

Day 25

Claire found us in the family room at around 4AM. She brought us bagels and cream cheese, and encouraged us to rest. Red-eyed and exhausted, we thanked her, and let her bring Talia back to her own room. Rich and I stayed in the family room for a couple of hours and slept.

When we returned to Talia's room, Rich picked her up and snuggled with her in the rocking chair. She was in the crook of one of his arms, and I was resting on his other arm. We allowed our eyes to close, trying once again to recharge ourselves. Instinctively though, I opened my eyes and noticed that Talia looked horrible. Her lips were losing their color, her face was turning grayish. Panic overwhelmed me.

I screamed, "Honey, I think she's dying!" I jumped out of my chair and ran to the open area where a team of doctors and nurses were performing their morning rounds. "Someone, help us, quick! Our baby is dying!" I shouted. No one seemed to move fast enough. Hysteria set in. In the 10 seconds that I was gone from her room, Talia somehow recovered. She was back to normal again, alive and pink. This is insane.

The doctors must think I am a lunatic. We have a "Do Not Resuscitate" order for Talia, but there I was, a maniac running around, trying to find someone to save her. It was then that one of the doctors suggested we go home and get some rest. This might take longer than they originally thought. I fear I will lose all my strength completely as time slowly ticks by.

Remember your source of strength.

Before we left Talia's room, we gave the nurses my parents' phone number and our beeper number in case they needed to reach us. I pray that they won't need to. As guilty as I sometimes feel leaving Talia, especially knowing that she doesn't have much time left, we desperately need a break.

We went to my parents' house (our "command central") to see Ariana, to give everyone an update, and for some respite before we returned to our emotional chaos at the hospital.

It was so good to see Ariana! Feeling her little bear hugs around my neck and hearing her whisper, "Mommy, I wuv you" warmed my heart. She asked about her baby sister. "Is she with God yet, Mommy?"

At two-and-a-half, Ari seems to be handling this extremely well. Since she is spending much of her time with my parents and sisters, I'm hoping that this experience won't leave her with any emotional scars. While she still seems her usually happy, bubbly self, during the last few days, she has had many wetting accidents. Much to my chagrin, I've overreacted to them. I feel horrible about it. I could blame it on my raw nerves, but it's more from feeling out of control altogether. I sometimes feel as though I am failing as a parent, failing both Talia and Ariana. I imagine that Ari's accidents are just her way of telling us that she doesn't like the current state of our lives very much either. So, of course, that's when guilt sets in. I feel guilty about leaving Talia to see Ariana; I feel guilty about leaving Ari to spend all my time with

Talia. I know I am doing the best I possibly can, given the circumstances. I have to let go of this guilt, but I'm not sure how.

When guilt makes its way into your heart, it blocks the flow of love in and out. Take the yoke off your shoulders, and release it to Me.

"God, please take this guilt from me and replace it with love, for myself as a mother, for my children, for everyone surrounding me," I pray. Moments later, peace fills my heart, just as I'd heard about so long ago.

We journey back here to Beth Israel this afternoon. Many of our friends come in with their kids to meet Talia. As I observe them looking at Talia, my curious mind wonders what they are thinking. Are they counting their blessings that their own children are healthy? Are they apprehensive about holding Talia, fearing the angel of death hovers nearby? I keep these thoughts to myself. I appreciate that we have a loving circle of friends who support us.

When the last of the visitors leave after 9:30PM, we are relieved that we can finally be alone with Talia again. It is as if we needed to soak in every living moment that she has left. At 11:00PM we went back to stay at my parents' house, since they live closer to the hospital than we do. We arrived back at their house at 11:30, and we watched some TV to unwind before going to bed. We were truly exhausted, both physically and emotionally.

Fifteen minutes later, the phone rang, and our hearts dropped! Who on earth would be calling at quarter to midnight? It had to be the hospital. It was. It was Claire.

"Sandy, Talia is having a hard time keeping her heart rate up and her color is starting to fade. We think you should come in."

My parents woke from the ringing of the phone. We hysterically told them that we had to go back, because Talia was about to die. They hugged us tightly and wished us luck. What else could one say? In silence, with our hearts and minds racing, we sped back there, to the hospital, which is about a half hour away. The only panicked thought that rushed through my mind was that we might not make it in time.

PLEASE DEAR GOD, DON'T LET HER DIE YET!

Fourteen

We anxiously arrived back in Talia's room 25 minutes later, not knowing what to expect. When we walked in, there was no pandemonium, only Claire and another nurse calmly watching over our beautiful, healthy looking daughter. She was as pink as she looked the last time we saw her and she was breathing comfortably. Claire explained that Talia appeared very close to death, grayish from a prolonged spell of apnea, but spontaneously recovered before we arrived. I feel instantly relieved, and can't wait to cradle her in my arms where she belongs. What a nasty scare she gave us.

A few moments later, as I was rocking her, I mockingly scolded her, "Talia, don't ever do that to us again." Suddenly, she looked strange. Her breathing became heavier, the color from her face and especially her lips was slowly fading. She sounded as if she was gasping for air. Her monitor started beeping a foreboding sound, which meant that her heart rate was dropping rapidly.

"Oh, Claire, look at her!" I cried. "What's happening to her?"

"Talia's having another episode of apnea. This may be the end," Claire said calmly.

Rich and I began to cry and hugged Talia fiercely, saying our good-byes. "We love you, Talia. We'll always love you and we'll miss you!" My heart ached.

Suddenly, the beeping stopped. Talia's color returned. Her heartrate is normal. We have mentally prepared ourselves, as best as one can, for the fact that she is going to die. Now everything has changed. The wide range of emotions that has swept through us in these last 30 minutes included sadness, fear, grief, joy, relief, frustration, but most of all, such confusion.

"I don't know how much longer I can keep going on this emotional roller coaster, Sandy," Rich said. "If we are here at the hospital when Talia passes away, then we'll be blessed. But if we aren't here, perhaps it wasn't meant to be. Can you live with that?"

I realized that we really have little control here, short of living at the hospital. "Yes, I can live with that." Accepting the fact that this is out of our control may offer us both some semblance of peace.

I wonder when we'll be able to reestablish some sense of normalcy in our lives, whatever that means. These false alarms are creating frantic twists and turns that are slowly draining our life energy. Oh, God, what is going on here? Why is this happening? Are we being tested?

> *There are no "tests" as you see them, although many people imagine that I throw out a "test" to see if one would pass or fail. My love is unconditional; there is no judgment on any of you. I simply encourage your soul to evolve, if you so choose. I cannot force you to evolve, since you were all given free will. As for Talia, she is simply exercising her free will. When her soul is ready, it will choose to leave, and that is when she will die. You see, Talia's soul has not completely finished its business. When it has, she will be ready to move on.*

Day 26

I feel as if I have major roles in two distinctly different plays at the same time. I need to adapt to each role in a heartbeat. The scenery is entirely different, as is the plot. In the hospital play, emotions run rampant and my senses are on overload. My ears listen for the heartrate alarm. My eyes check Talia's lips for a change of color. My food has no flavor, for my mind is elsewhere. My words include medical terms that I now understand. My skin feels cold, as if death is nearby.

In the home play, I can hear the birds singing harmoniously in the fruit trees in our front yard. I watch Ariana playing happily with her blocks on the living room floor. I savor my oversized mug of warm, sweet Red Rose tea in the morning. I feel the fresh, warm breeze, nudging us to play outside. When I am engrossed in one play, it is sometimes hard to remember that the other also exists. I am confused as to which one is real.

This morning, I chose to be in the home play to clean the house and play with Ari. We picked up some pictures that we took over the last few weeks. Talia and Ari, Talia and her cousins, Talia alone. It is so hard to believe that she isn't going to be with us always.

This afternoon I switch roles for the hospital play. A physical therapist comes in to evaluate Talia, though why, at this late date, I don't understand. She's trying to elicit some response from Talia. Talia never responds to our voices. Nor does she blink in the rare instances where her eyes are open and we slowly move one of our hands toward her face or back and forth in front of her face. We think she may be blind and deaf. It doesn't surprise me now when she barely responds for the physical therapist. Then the physical therapist asks me to try the same exercises that she has just performed — slowly moving Talia's arm up and down, talking to her at the same time. She notes that Talia responds more to my touch and handling. Thanks, Talia, you do know I'm here. What a blessing! As happy as that makes me feel, I am also aware of a sick feeling in my stomach. Are we giving up on her too soon? Fear votes "yes." The voice of my soul reassures me, "no."

I spoke to Claire at length about Talia's uncertain future. Based on her prior experience without a respirator, they obviously think she is going to die sooner rather than later. But now that she seems to be doing pretty well, no one really knows when she is going to die. She might survive the newborn period. I ask Claire what our options are, if Talia continues to live like this. She explains that no one is pressing us to make a decision. However, at some point, we will have two choices to make: either place Talia in a chronic care facility (visiting whenever we'd like), or take her home to die. Neither option eases my mind, but I feel absolutely certain that if she isn't going to die and be with God in the very near future, she belongs at home with us.

Rich came in about an hour later, and the three of us continued this increasingly heated discussion. Unfortunately, Rich and I don't agree on which option is best. He has a totally different view. He is adamantly opposed to bringing Talia home. He's worried about the quality of our life at home, especially for Ariana's sake. Would she get the attention she needs from me if all my energy is with Talia? From my point of view, there is no room for negotiation. As close as Rich and I have become through this whole ordeal, if anything is going to break us down and tear us apart, it is going to be this decision, because I'm not budging. I just can't. Claire reassures us that there is no clear-cut right or wrong decision. The hospital will allow us whatever time we need to make our decision.

Day 27

Rich and I have agreed to disagree for the time being. We rode home in silence last night. I sat and prayed, "God, you know that this is a trying time for Rich and me. Please help us to feel your love surrounding us. Help us to work through each step of this journey together with love in our hearts." Almost immediately, I sensed that we'd be okay.

In our phone update this morning, one of the nurses reports that Talia remained stable through the night, although she has had more episodes of apnea and bradycardia, in which she stops breathing and her heart stops beating. Because of this, Dr. Stewart started testing her "cap gas" level. This measures the amount of carbon dioxide building up in her blood-stream. Testing her level serves as an indicator of how effectively (or ineffectively) she breathes. A normal level is between 30 and 40. Talia's level today was at 59. They conclude that her carbon dioxide level was rising at a slow rate and that her deterioration could be very slow. What a way to describe a child's death.

I spent the whole day with Ariana, trying to recapture what has been lost between us during this time. She is so energetic, so full of life. Since last week, Rich went back to work, mostly for half days to get his mind off Talia's situation for a short time. We haven't talked about Talia since last night's discussion. We were planning to return to the hospital later.

On our ride in, Rich said he'd been thinking all day about last night's conversation. He decided that he also wants Talia to be home with us, if she continues to live. How did he change his mind so quickly? Thank you, God, for Rich. I can't make it through this without him.

When we arrive at the hospital, Talia is not in her room. We are convinced that something has happened to her. Then we hear Claire call out to us from the other room.

"Hi guys, Talia's over here with me. I didn't want her to be lonely, so I brought her with me on my rounds."

Right next to Claire was Talia in a battery-operated swing. She was sleeping so contentedly in a new outfit that I didn't recognize. It was a pretty green, flowered jumpsuit with a matching cap.

"Claire, what's that she's wearing?" I asked.

"I know I'm not supposed to get so involved, but I saw this adorable outfit at the store, and had to buy it for Talia. She spit up on her other outfit. I hope you don't mind that I put this one on her."

There is no better feeling than knowing that Talia is being lovingly taken care of even when we aren't here. Rich and I feel an incredible bond with Claire. We are so thankful that she is in our lives. And we are grateful for the lightness that is in the air tonight. We needed it.

On the way home, I asked Rich, "If Talia was so abnormal right from the very beginning as a little embryo, why didn't I just have another miscarriage? Why would we have to go through all this pain?" No sooner did the words come out of my mouth than my heart sensed the answer.

Before he had a chance to respond, I spoke up again. "Never mind, I think I already know."

"Well, could you fill me in then?" Rich said.

"Rich, I just *know* deep down inside that there is so much more to our experience than the birth of an unhealthy child," I replied. "Even though she didn't develop normally right from conception, if I had miscarried, we would never have gotten the chance to know her and love her, even if it was for a short amount of time. And look at all the wonderful people we've gotten to know, and all the love that we've felt. This whole experience absolutely confirms my belief that there are gems to be found within every challenge if we look for them, and that we're placed here to learn and to love and to grow. Talia has placed her footprints on our hearts. I don't know about you, but I know I've been changed forever."

He nodded in agreement, but he didn't say a word. I sensed that he felt the same.

When we got home, I felt the urge to write again. It was as if there was something bubbling up from deep within me that had to be expressed. From my pen came these words:

> The process of grieving takes much longer than anyone
> expects. There are varied emotions that one must go through
> But each one, if truly felt, will help to cleanse you enough so
> that you can move on through the process. Some people
> squelch a certain feeling, thus preventing this process from
> being fully completed. This is why there are so many unre-
> solved conflicts raging in people's minds — because their
> true feelings are not completely processed. They then carry
> that emotional baggage around with them in all situations
> of their lives. Their ultimate outlook on life is therefore jaded.

> Sometimes it can be scary to face what is the truth in your
> life, but when you do, pure light can shine through, and
> help you to fully experience each moment. Death is a
> natural process which leads to ultimate enlightenment. Do
> not be fearful, for those who have gone are entirely at peace
> and completely surrounded by love.

"....those who have gone are entirely at peace and completely surrounded by love." What a beautiful image that conjured up in my mind, of angels surrounding those who have passed on with total love. As I finished this writing that came "through" me, I felt completely surrounded and lovingly protected by a divine presence that was watching over me. This immediate sense of inner peace permeated any grief or sadness in the moment, and it helped me to feel entirely whole.

Rereading the words helps me momentarily forget that we are in a lot of pain. I feel strongly that we can and will survive. And I know that I will someday draw upon this experience to help others through their pain.

Fifteen

Day 29

July 21

A black binder in Talia's room contains all the nurses' notes from every shift. I like to read it from time to time, because it contains vital statistics, visitors, feedings, and observations. I don't understand all the abbreviations. Today Talia's notes state, "She is overall physically well..." Physically well? How can she be physically well? She's dying. Then I read on, "...albeit neurologically devastated." Neurologically devastated. It is such a dramatic way to describe a newborn, especially our newborn. But it is the truth. And I've learned very recently that one needs to face the truth in order to move forward in life.

> When one turns away from the truth, they are merely prolonging what they need to face at some point for their soul's growth. The truth will always present itself again and again, yet it is up to each individual when and if they choose to face it. The truth can and does set one free...from fear. Make a pledge to yourself. Follow the truth. It shall lead you to the path of peace.

We had a family meeting with the care team this afternoon to discuss long-term options for Talia. We reiterated our intentions to bring Talia home, if she doesn't die in the near future.

The social worker suggested that we consider family counseling, if Talia continues to live. I expressed that I felt as though we've already been through it during these last few weeks! I've never in my life dug so deeply to express my emotions as I have with the nurses here at Beth Israel. I said that I didn't feel like I was in denial about Talia's impending death. I've held back no tears or feelings.

At this moment, I feel peaceful about our decisions. Perhaps denial is staring me right in the face. I still don't think so.

The only type of counseling we have had on our minds is genetic counseling. There is still such uncertainty about her diagnosis. The possibility exists that her condition is genetic. Rich and I have talked about whether we'll ever have the courage to have another child. It is far too premature to think about that, but we've decided that we'll both undergo genetic testing, if and when we want to have another child. Dr. Stewart explained that Talia's condition is a one-in-a-million rarity — a fluke of nature. Something happened at the very cellular level of her development, and the chance that it would happen again is exceptionally slim. I don't care. I've also heard of people getting struck by lightning twice. And I didn't know how well they survived.

This afternoon, as we spent time alone with Talia, Rich and I discussed issues that need resolution. The first is what to do with the birth announcements I had already picked up from the printer. For the last few weeks, we've been in a quandary about whether to send them out or not. Initially, we wanted to wait until she came home to send them out. Then, when we realized that she may not come home at all, we didn't know what to do. Is it appropriate? Would it make people feel uncomfortable? We've decided today that we *have* to send them out. We are so proud of our little Talia and want to show her off to the world. Accompanying the announcements will be reprints of a beautiful picture of Ariana sitting on this rocking chair in her room holding Talia. The look in Ari's big brown eyes is precious. In the picture, she's beaming with love and pride as she holds her baby sister in her arms.

Another issue is cremation versus burial for Talia. Neither option sounds appealing, if I allow myself to think about the process. So I force myself to focus on my belief that her physical shell will die, but her spirit, her soul, her essence, lives on. She'll forever be surrounded by God's love and light.

I recall a television movie I once saw about 20 years ago with Richard Thomas (John-boy Walton). In this movie, Richard's character was consoling his young son after his mother died from cancer. He was explaining to his son what happens when someone dies. He held up a large glove. "When a person is born," he said, "their spirit enters their body and gives their body life." He placed his hand into the glove and wiggled his fingers to give the glove life. "When their life is over, their spirit leaves their body." He then took his hand out of the glove. "The body is then an empty shell, but the spirit lives on forever," he said, as he held the empty glove in one hand and wiggled his other fingers in the air.

That image is still with me, and it helps me now as I grapple with issues surrounding Talia's impending death. We need to find what is the most comforting to us, and we decide on cremation. And we want her gray dinosaur to be cremated with her. We also start discussing a funeral service. More than focusing solely on her death, we want her memorial service to celebrate her life. The image that immediately pops into my mind is of pink balloons, floating up to Talia with love.

Day 30

Talia seems to be getting fed up with her daily routine. Whenever the nurses insert the nasal feeding tube, Talia seems very irritated, makes strident sounds, and turns dusky in color. She has also been spitting up after her feedings, which is unusual for her. The explanation is that the reflex mechanism in her stomach might be breaking down, not allowing Talia to tolerate her formula. This indicates that she may be close to the end. The end of her physical existence, perhaps, but I am becoming more and more convinced that nothing ever comes to an end. For one ending is merely another beginning. It's all a process, this journey called life. And in a short time, we've learned to treasure every moment of it — the smells, the sights, the touches.

Why does it have to take a crisis for us to learn this? I sense the answer — we probably wouldn't choose to learn it on our own.

> *And because pain often reawakens one to one's senses again, and to this journey called life.*

Later this afternoon, a different doctor came to see us at Talia's bedside. He explained that because she is vomiting more frequently, there now exists an increased threat of fluid collecting in her lungs. She might develop pneumonia. He reminded us that the course of action will be to administer comfort, not lifesaving measures. Therefore, traditional antibiotics will not be given in case of an infection. They could give her narcotics, which he promised will eliminate any discomfort she may experience.

In the confines of my mind, a raging battle is brewing.

My maternal instinct seems to scream, "You call yourself a mother? How could you just sit back and watch your daughter die? Forget about the 'Do Not Resuscitate' order, GIVE HER THE ANTIBIOTICS if she needs it. You need to SAVE HER LIFE!"

In response, my soul gently whispers, "It's out of your control, let her go, with love."

We agreed that narcotics will be used, if necessary. Since when did my soul get so smart? Probably when I reconnected with God.

Talia has had more friends and relatives coming in to meet her and to say good-bye. I often wonder about the conversations they have when they leave her room. By the end of tonight, Rich and I are exhausted. Because we've had visitors here for most of the day, Rich is feeling badly that he hasn't gotten to spend much time with Talia. The nurses say that we have to learn how to set boundaries with our friends, so we will have enough time alone with Talia. I don't know how to tell people not to visit, nor do I want to. It seems easier to forget the painful reality when there are more people around. I usually feel emotional when I am alone with Talia. I could be gently rocking with her in total peace one minute; the very next, fearfully clutching her, crying hysterically, and pleading with her not to die. So much for facing the truth.

Day 31

July 23

Rich and I seem to be taking things more in stride. We don't panic if Talia spits up on one of us after her feeding. If she has a seizure (or turns slightly blue) while I hold her, I remain totally calm. I have no idea why. Are we finally accepting and hardening ourselves to the grim reality that we'll soon lose Talia?

> *Perhaps not hardened, but healed. Acceptance is the first step to healing. You've accepted her condition, because you've realized there is a larger plan than what you can see.*

Talia now vomits after almost every feeding. The nurses think that perhaps there is too much stimulation at the time of her feedings. They started to darken her room and try to be quiet while they insert her nasal tube and feed her. They're very sweet and thoughtful. I feel thankful for these wonderful people, whom we would not have met had Talia been a healthy newborn.

Rich stayed home with Ariana tonight, so I have a solid three hours to be alone with Talia before I head home. I had brought in a radio a few days ago, so I put on some soft music. This is heaven. I snuggle with my little Sleeping Beauty on my chest, and there is no fear present — only love. As I rock with Talia, I ask the nurse on duty about local support groups for parents whose babies have died. Not only do I want a network of support, I also sense a need to start reaching out to help others in any way I can. Perhaps it will be a way to help me keep Talia's memory alive and bring added meaning to this tremendous life challenge.

> *When one's heart is ready, reaching out to help and to be helped by others will always shed new light and add a new level of meaning after a challenge in life. With the added degrees of understanding, you will be able to see any painful experience as an opportunity for healing and growth.*

Sixteen

Day 32

Late this morning, we arrived at the hospital with Ariana. As most children do, she always has such a wonderful way of staying present in the moment, finding joy in every situation! She squeals with delight whenever she rides in the elevator. And when we agree to buy her those homemade chocolate-chip cookies from the cafeteria, one would think we have given her the world. Perhaps I should look more to her for my life lessons!

> *Children are the best teachers of all, because they still have something that many adults have chosen to overlook...*
> *their innocence.*

My parents came to visit us shortly after we arrived. My mother looked especially pretty this morning, wearing a brand new, navy blue pantsuit. For a change of scenery, we brought Talia to the family room after she was fed. I was watching a beautiful picture, trying to imprint it into my memory. My mother was proudly holding her newest (twelfth) grandchild. Ariana was trying to teach Talia "The Itsy Bitsy Spider." In a split second, however, everything changed. Talia vomited all over my mother, and started gagging, turning blue. As quickly as it had drained from her, though, Talia's color was restored. My mother remained quite calm through this mini ordeal, but Ariana was frightened and began to cry. I was alarmed, because Talia has now been vomiting after every feeding. To me, it is a constant reminder of her dismal life.

After we cleaned up, my parents left and brought Ariana home with them, so Rich and I could have some quiet time with Talia. I feel desperate in my attempt to memorize her as she is at this moment. I never want to forget every inch of her, the fuzzy little hair on her shoulders and back, her innocent baby smell, the soft wrinkles of her skin, her dark curly hair, her warmth as she lay on my chest. She truly is our little angel.

Emotionally exhausted, we finally leave the hospital at 7:00PM. We agree that Ariana would stay overnight with my parents. My gut is telling me that Talia doesn't have much time left. I want to get an early start back to the hospital before the morning traffic becomes heavy.

When we got home, I lay down on my bed and reflected on how much has happened in our lives in the last month. Would we ever have some semblance of normalcy? Am I selfish to be thinking about it? I miss the wonders of having a newborn at home, I miss being able to focus my attention solely on Ariana, and I miss talking and laughing with Rich.

Even though the events of this past month have been out of my control, I still feel guilty that I am unable to keep it all together. God, please help us all to find peace soon.

At about 8:45, I decided to address the birth announcement envelopes while watching TV. An hour later, halfway through the mailing list, panic flashed through my mind. What if Talia dies before we mail these? My pen was moving furiously; I HAD to hurry up and get these out before she dies. Ten minutes later, our phone rang. Terror bristled through my body.

"Talia is having severe difficulty breathing. Her condition is rapidly deteriorating. We think you should come in immediately, " a nurse from Beth Israel said.

I screamed out to the next room where Rich was exercising.

"RICH, WE'VE GOT TO GO NOW!"

We had a forty-five minute drive to the hospital. Every second that ticked by was torturous. I had to see my baby before she died! Sitting in the car, imagining Talia dying alone, was almost too much to bear. "GET ME OUT OF THIS CAR," I wanted to scream, but I had to stay calm for Rich's sake so we could get there in one piece. I felt a palpable combination of fear and anxiety, not knowing what we were about to face. There was nothing I can do but pray, "God, please get us there safely, and let Talia hold on until we arrive."

Thirty-five minutes later, we finally reached the hospital.

As we ran through the main door, the security guard tried to stop us. "Where are you…"

"Let us go. Our baby is dying upstairs; we've got to get there quick!" Rich shouted angrily. The elevator made an express trip to her floor. Rich and I, clutching each other's hands, ran at full speed from the elevator to her room. One of the nurses was holding Talia, whose gray dinosaur was tucked snugly into the crook of her arm.

Choking on my tears, I tried to ask, "Has she…?" I couldn't finish.

The nurse wiped away her own tears. "Talia's already on her way to heaven. She passed away five minutes before you got here."

Rich and I both sobbed as we looked at our precious little angel. "Can we…hold her?" I asked. I was almost afraid to hold her, but Talia looked nothing like the picture of death that was firmly planted in my imagination. She was still pink and warm. She looked more peaceful and beautiful than we had ever seen her.

"I love you Talia. You will always be in my heart. Thank you for being our little angel. We will never, ever forget you."

Rich and I took turns holding her and rocking her. Fifteen minutes later, we were surprised to see Claire walk into Talia's room. It was her night off, but she had instructed the hospital to call her if Talia should die. Claire asked if she could hold Talia. As she held her, she wept and said her own final good-byes. Soon, Mary, one of the nurse practitioners with whom we were also close, came in on *her* night off to say good-bye. We have had such caring and loving support at this hospital. Talia came into the world embraced with love, and she made her final departure surrounded by love as well. In the midst of our raw emotions, we all felt an odd sense of peace in the room — for Talia. She was now free of the physical limitations that have bound her during her short stay on earth.

And this process has stripped you of many emotional
limitations that have bound you in the past.

After a few hours, we felt it was time to go. We thanked the nurse who had held Talia while she died. Though we weren't physically there for Talia when she died, we were comforted by the fact that she was surrounded by love and protected by her little dinosaur.

Rich and I both felt a deep emptiness as we walked out of Talia's room for the last time. Our makeshift world at Beth Israel's NICU had provided us with a comfortable safety net for the past 31 days. When we stepped out of this hospital door, it would be torn away. Now what? It scared me to think about facing the real world without Talia.

How do you put the pieces of your life back together after the death of a child? How do you survive? I know that there is immeasurable pain to be felt, but I also know that, somehow we'll survive.

Sometimes, the most important pieces of your life's puzzle
come to you after a long haul.

Seventeen

I've stopped counting the days, because they don't matter anymore. What I'm beginning to sense is that the only way one can put a life together again after any challenge is moment by moment, piece by piece.

We are so thankful for Ariana, our bright little light. When we told her that Talia died, her response was, "Oh." How can she really comprehend what was happening? She's only two and a half. I believe that children build their response to challenging life events by taking their cues from their parents or other caregivers. At times, Ariana clings to my side, which I cherish. At other times, she talks nonstop about Talia, which I also love. "Mommy, what is Talia eating up in heaven? Can she hear us?" At lunch today, Ari looked at me with her big brown eyes. "Mommy, when is Talia coming back *down* from heaven?" she said seriously. It broke my heart to tell her that she's not coming back, but her spirit will always be with us. As I spoke these words, I was hoping that she'd understand. I am also hoping that I will understand.

We're planning Talia's memorial service for June 27th, and we're keeping ourselves busy by taking care of all the details. Trips to the church, the florist, the funeral parlor. Each stop brings fresh tears as we repeatedly discuss our plans for this celebration of Talia's life. It all seems so unnatural to be making these arrangements for an infant! Everyone we've encountered has been wonderfully supportive.

I was emotionally exhausted when we got home and felt compelled to take a break from it all. The best way I know is through my writing. Here's what came flowing onto the paper:

> *Talia is at peace with herself; proud of what she has been able to accomplish in such a short period of time. She was more advanced than she appeared on the outside. Her spirit was able to touch many people because there was a need. She is happy with herself (at this point, I imagined that her spirit was dancing!), knowing she's brought such joy to so many people. She will continue to bring forth new lessons to those who are willing to see them.*

> *Go forth and try to open others' perspectives so that they can be enriched by your experience. The pain throughout this past journey can be lessened by the knowledge that it was done entirely through love. Through pain emerges new growth, which you have realized. You must help others through their pain. You have the ability and the words to do so. Work through this, to experience all that life is now offering you. Truly experience life — by playing, loving, and learning. Each day offers new beauty, should you choose to see it. And you are now at the point where you can look past the physicality of things and people, and see their true beauty within. This is a gift from Talia.*

The phrase, "It was done entirely through love." This phrase jumps off the page at me. That's it! Could it be that Talia *chose* to be born to us to teach us lessons? Could it be that her one-in-a-million disorder wasn't some cruel joke? Was it a gift to help us grow spiritually and emotionally? Did her soul truly choose this lifetime out of love for us? After this last writing, I feel an overwhelming need to share this message. So many people were missing the point — and I almost did too. There was a life to be celebrated. We experienced much more than a birth and a death. We experienced a spiritual awakening.

I showed Rich what I had just written and explained that something was urging me to speak at Talia's memorial service, perhaps to read what was written through me in the last couple of weeks. He's so sweet and protective; he probably thought that it was merely an impulsive reaction. "Sandy, honey, you're going to be very *emotional* that day. Think twice about it. I don't think you should do it," he said softly.

There are times in life when it is important to listen to another's advice for you, and there are times when your own inner wisdom is far too strong to ignore. Quite often in my life, I've been easily swayed by Rich's opinions, thinking he was wiser. This is one of those times, however, when I have to follow my intuition, my inner knowing. It's telling me that I have to deliver a message — not for me, but for Talia, and most importantly, for God. The thought makes me feel surprisingly excited. The same type of excitement you feel when you are about to deliver a present to someone you love.

Rich and I spent the entire afternoon satisfying a sudden compulsion to clean. We were going to have everyone to our home after the memorial service, and Rich and I were on a mission. I tackled every nook and cranny of the inside of the house, while Rich weeded and planted beds of flowers. He also got our brand new sun room ready for tomorrow. We had a three season room built onto the back of our house. This sun room will always remind me of Talia. It came into our lives the same time she did. It was started while I was still pregnant with Talia, and was finished just a few days ago. The interior hasn't been painted yet and the tile floor wasn't down yet, so Rich put down some green indoor/outdoor carpet to get us through tomorrow. Our work today seemed therapeutic, partly because it kept us occupied, but more so, I think, because it was giving us a sense of control at a time when we felt we had very little.

Some of my sisters were wondering whether their kids, who are four to eight, were too young to go to Talia's service. Their concern was that it will be too sad for them, that it would be hard to explain. We've already decided that we want Ariana to be there with us. It's important for everyone to make their own decisions, but I believe strongly that death is a part of life. To shield kids from that is to shield them from life. They ultimately decided they would bring their kids to the service. My heart is happy.

Every time I think about speaking at Talia's service, sudden rushes of weakness and nausea sweep through my body. But, almost immediately, a sense of deep serenity is restored within me, as I remember that I am on a mission from God. How odd it is, to feel such a dichotomy of emotions. Luckily, the inner peace sustains me.

I told a few people that I was going to speak at Talia's service. They wonder how I will keep myself together. I don't know either, but I do know that God is supporting me and filling me with love and understanding. At other times in my life, if I forced myself to be strong during a challenge, I'd crumble like a leaf. But now, when I take quiet time for myself, I can feel healing love strengthen me. My writing makes me feel alive once again. This came through this afternoon:

> With the passing of each day comes opportunities and challenges. Some do not seek to look at events in their lives as opportunities or challenges. Instead they see what they want to see-they see misfortune and grief. When one can look beyond the outward appearance of life's events and see the true meaning and purpose of what's being unveiled to them, their lives can be redirected onto the road to further purposefulness.

Look to each day to try and find the speck of beauty —
whether it be a ray of sunshine or a bird singing, or a
friend's voice. There are so many miracles surrounding you
that you tend to overlook. Keep a log or journal of the one
thing you've learned each day or the miracle you've observed.
These pearls of wisdom can be your guide in the future, and
can offer you solace during your times of sadness.

Well, my miracle is the higher power behind the calming, soothing words that come through in my writing. Thank you, God, I'm developing a need for your strength.

It's about...

"It's about time," I heard within my heart.

Later that night in bed, Rich again reassured me. "Sandy, it's all right if you don't have the courage to speak at Talia's service tomorrow. You don't have to prove anything to anyone. I believe that these messages are helping us, and that's good enough for me."

"Rich, I really feel that the last four years of teaching the Dale Carnegie course (for public speaking) were preparing me for this one moment. And I very strongly feel Talia's spirit right here on my right shoulder saying, 'C'mon, Mommy, you can do it!' " I know that I will.

As I drifted off to sleep, I prayed, "God, please let your loving presence surround me tomorrow. I know I'll need it."

My presence is with you always. Choose to feel it.

Eighteen

Today was the day of Talia's memorial service. Everything seemed to go in slow motion this morning — getting Ariana ready, and trying to find an outfit for me to wear. I picked out my favorite royal blue suit with thin colorful stripes. The skirt didn't quite fit yet, so I zippered it as high as I could, and prayed it would stay up. Before we left for the church, Rich surprised me and Ariana with gifts. He gave Ari guardian angel earrings, and he gave me a necklace with two delicate charms — an angel and the letter "T". He is so thoughtful. I promised him that anytime I needed strength, I'd hold onto the charms.

The day started out cloudy and dreary, just like our emotions. However, just as we were leaving for the church, the clouds broke open. Bright sunshine filled the sky. This to me was a sign that God's love was with me, and that I was doing the right thing.

We arrived early to make sure everything was set up the way we wanted. Fresh pink and white flowers adorned the church. Because many of the people there had never seen our little angel, we had framed pictures of Talia on display as people walked up the stairs of the church, as well as on the altar. We also brought Talia's birth announcements, which we never did have the chance to mail, along with the copies we'd made of the picture of Ari and Talia together. People could take one of each as they walked into the sanctuary. Talia's spirit was definitely there.

The church was packed with individuals from many chapters of our lives; our families and their children, friends, Rich's current work associates, co-workers from our past jobs, college friends from different states, Claire and other members of Talia's care team, and neighbors. It was a heartwarming sight to see all the love that surrounded us.

Many people were moved to tears as they walked in and saw the pictures and birth announcements. Then, Reverend Paul opened the service with some poignant words. The associate minister read the following poem that I had found in a Make-A-Wish newsletter years ago, when Rich and I were volunteers before we had our own children. The poem struck a chord with me back then, and I had saved it, never expecting to have it read at my own daughter's service.

Thy Will be Done

I'll lend you for a little while a child of mine, God said.
For you to love the while she lives and mourn for when she's dead.
It may be six or seven years, seventeen or sixty-three.
But will you 'til I call her back, take care of her for me?

She'll bring her charms to gladden you, and shall her stay be brief,
You'll have her lovely memories as solace for your grief.
I cannot promise she will stay, since all from earth return,
But there are lessons taught down there, I want this child to learn.

I've looked the whole world over in my search for teachers true
And from the throngs that crowd life's lanes, I have selected you.
Now, will you give her all your love, nor think the labor vain
Or hate me when I come to take her home with me again.

I fancied that I hear them say, Dear Lord, Thy will be done,
For all the joy that she shall bring, the risk of grief we'll run.
We'll shelter her with tenderness, we'll love her while we may,
And, for the happiness we've known, forever grateful stay.
But shall the angels call for her much sooner than we've planned,
We'll brave the bitter grief that comes and try to understand.

— Anonymous

Then it was time for my message. My heart pounded, yet I knew this was not about me; it was about a loving message from a divine source. The associate minister had a copy of what I was going to read, in case I changed my mind at the last minute or couldn't finish it. Deep down, I knew that I could deliver my message, rather God's message. What helped was once again sensing Talia's spirit encouraging me, "C'mon, Mommy, you can do it!" Rich squeezed my hand and whispered that he loved me. I held onto my new charms for a moment, then walked up to the pulpit.

Only a handful of people knew that I was going to do this, so when I walked up to the microphone, there was a look of horror on many faces. On the surface level, it probably was a sad picture — a mother about to speak about her small infant dying. But if you go beyond the surface of appearances, there was so much more that we had experienced. Most importantly, I felt that I was lovingly touched by God's loving spirit and by an angel named Talia. I thanked everyone for coming, and I began to read "A tribute to Talia", which combined the writings from July 16, 20 and 25...

A Tribute to Talia

The belief "there is a reason for all that happens" is valid.
The knowledge may not be revealed to you for many
months, years, or even longer, but feel that there is a higher
order working things through your lives. To have lost a child
is devastating, but you must look at the meaning of her life;
what she symbolizes. Talia was eager to be born unto you to
show you lessons in even just these four weeks. You have
learned quickly, and you will be able to carry these new-
found strengths with you forever. And they'll help you to
reach new heights of awareness in your life.

Do not look at her death as a sad time, but rejoice in her
spirit's presence in your life. So it should be with anyone
you encounter in your lives — to try and love as much as
possible, and learn from them. If you can keep yourselves
open to those two tasks in your daily lives, you can find
freedom from that which burdens most people. Your lives
can be fulfilling to an even greater degree by keeping yourselves open. As difficult as this process has been for both of
you, feel blessed that you have been able to experience it.
You were chosen because of your ability to learn from it.
Remember Talia not for what she could never be, but for
how she helped enrich your lives and the lives around you.

The process of grieving takes much longer than anyone
expects. There are varied emotions that one must go
through. But each one, if truly felt, will help to cleanse you
enough so that you can move on through the process. Some
people squelch a certain feeling, thus preventing this process
from being fully completed. This is why there are so many
unresolved conflicts raging in people's minds — because

their true feelings are not completely processed. They then carry that emotional baggage around with them in all situations of their lives. Their ultimate outlook on life is therefore jaded. Sometimes it can be scary to face what is the truth in your life, but when you do, pure light can shine through, and help you to fully experience each moment. Death is a natural process which leads to ultimate enlightenment. Do not be fearful, for those who have gone are entirely at peace and completely surrounded by love.

Talia is at peace with herself; proud of what she has been able to accomplish in such a short period of time. She was more advanced than she appeared on the outside. Her spirit was able to touch many people because there was a need. She is happy with herself, knowing she's brought such joy to so many people. She will continue to bring forth new lessons to those who are willing to see them.

Go forth and try to open others' perspectives so that they can be enriched by your experience. The pain throughout this past journey can be lessened by the knowledge that it was done entirely through love. Through pain emerges new growth, which you have realized. You must help others through their pain. You have the ability and the words to do so. Work through this, to experience all that life is now offering you. Truly experience life — by playing, loving, and learning. Each day offers new beauty, should you choose to see it. And you are now at the point where you can look past the physicality of things and people, and see their true beauty within. This is a gift from Talia.

Every time I spoke Talia's name, my voice cracked and tears welled up in my eyes, but I slowly paused and redirected myself. As I looked out into the audience, I tried to look past the sad, teary faces that I saw. I focused on reaching their hearts and souls as I delivered the message.

I did it. "Thank you, Talia, thank you, God, for helping me get through what was probably one of the proudest moments of my life," I silently prayed. When I sat down, there was a rush of indescribable serenity, knowing that I had trusted my instinct and followed the spirit of God. It was a wonderful feeling.

One that you will hopefully choose to know more about in the years to come.

Rich and I greeted each and every individual as they left the sanctuary. Tears of sadness, of grief, and of joy from seeing our loved ones continually flowed. Many people came up to us with such sorrow in their eyes and said, "We're *so* sorry for you," or "It was a blessing that she died." I didn't want people to say they were sorry for us. I wanted them to say, "What a beautiful blessing that you had Talia for a month. Congratulations on your angel. Congratulations on all your growth." I desperately wanted every person who was at the church to understand fully the meaning behind the tribute, that death is a part of life, and that there are lessons that can be learned through all situations. I wanted people to understand that this was not a horrible trick that happened to us, that it was all done through love. I wanted them to have a sense of the spiritual growth that had taken place within us. Could they *not* see it this way? Some were obviously touched right away, but I sensed that many still didn't understand. I felt frustrated and sorry that they didn't get it.

You've planted seeds. Let them grow.

Then I remembered my *own* words at every wake or funeral I've ever gone to. "I'm *so* sorry; I'm sorry for your loss," was my usual phrase. I knew nothing about learning any spiritual lessons from death, let alone much about spirituality in general, until I experienced that type of pain firsthand. It was then that I reopened the door to my spirituality. Who was I to judge anyone, when I'd acted and spoken as they did many times before? I've come to understand that lessons are hidden underneath any painful situation. And though some may readily see those "gems," others, usually those who are going through the pain, may not be ready to look for them. One chooses if and when one is ready, for each person is on his/her own path. We cannot force anyone to see a lesson; we can simply live the example. Quite often the clarity of these thoughts takes me by surprise.

Nearly every person told me that they had gained strength from Talia's tribute, which brought comfort to my heart. One friend told me that he was inspired to go home and start hugging his young daughter more because of today. Isn't it sad that we often wait until a crisis strikes a little too close to home to start treating our loved ones better?

I also thought it odd that people said that they wouldn't have had the strength or courage to speak as I did. I honestly saw no options. I believe that when we sense that God calls to us, it's in our highest and best interest to find a way to respond. I merely answered the call. While I was trying to run from my pain when Talia was alive, I wonder how many busy signals God received? Perhaps God had been trying to get my attention all along, to help me through my pain. I vow today to stay connected to my spiritual core. This means being open to the gentle nudgings within my heart and listening to the whispers within my soul — for that is how I sense God speaks to me.

As people walked out of the church, a few of my nieces and nephews handed out pink balloons. Most said a prayer for Talia, then released their pink balloon into the bright sky. Rich, Ariana, and I huddled in a small circle, saying our own prayers for Talia, as we clutched our balloons. Part of me wanted to hang on to them, as if they were a piece of Talia. It was a silly thought, and I let it go as we released the final three balloons. What a beautiful sight, all those pink balloons floating freely in the blue sky, each a heartfelt symbol of our love for her.

I was happy with Talia's service. It was exactly as I had envisioned, and my heart overflowed with love. We had invited everyone back to our house after the service. This would be our only chance to have a party in Talia's honor. It was unlike any party I would have wished for her — no ponies, no moon bouncers, no goodie bags, no candles on the cake, no pin-the-tail-on-the-donkey. In another lifetime, perhaps. This was truly a celebration of her life, a big party for our little angel. She is now our *true* angel, whose spirit will be near us forever.

Nineteen

There have been a myriad of challenges to face since Talia's death. Although there are brief periods of calmness, my emotions are still raw. There are many moments when I wonder if I'll ever be able to laugh or have the *desire* to be happy again. I sometimes feel as though I am losing my connection with the rest of the world, because I imagine that no one can understand the depths of the pain that I often feel. My family visits, friends call. But it's not enough. "I know how you feel," some say, "I was so sad when I lost my dad or my grandmother." I half-listen, wanting to scream, "NO, YOU DON'T KNOW HOW I FEEL UNLESS YOU'VE LOST A CHILD!" Losing a child defies the laws of nature. This emptiness is intense.

Sympathy cards have been arriving every day. Each time I get another card, I hold it to my heart before opening it, praying that it will contain some magic words that will connect with my heart and soul. But most of the cards say the same thing — a printed message about sorrow or grief. Nearly all are signed, "You're in our thoughts and prayers. Love…so and so." People must not realize that everybody signs sympathy cards the same way. After a while, it loses all meaning. At times I feel angry and bitter, wanting someone, or something, to take away some of this pain I feel. No one and no words on a card do it for me. There is a deep void that is excruciatingly hard to fill, except with sadness.

I went grocery shopping today for the first time since Talia died. I was walking through the supermarket that I have frequented for years. I wanted so badly for the employees to notice that I wasn't pregnant anymore. I wanted them to ask me the normal questions… "boy or girl…how big…what did you name it…?" But no one did. Everyone around me is living their lives as though nothing is wrong, while I'm struggling just to make it through each day, trying to avoid an emotional break-down! Don't they know what I've just been through? Doesn't anyone care?

I desperately need to talk about Talia — perhaps to keep her memory alive. What if I forget? Oh God, please don't let me forget her! How did I start sinking into the grief again like this? I thought I was handling this so well! God, where are you now, when I really need you? In times like these, out of sheer desperation, I get down on my knees and pray. Instant relief follows as I can always feel a loving spirit lift some of my pain. God, I'm sorry that I have forgotten to connect lately. Please help me to remember.

Rich has gone back to work. I'm envious that it is easy for him to "escape" it all. I'm having a hard time keeping my mind occupied. I had planned on being a stay-at-home mom for Ariana and Talia, but there is a baby missing from this idyllic picture. Between grief over missing Talia and postpartum blues, my hormones are on overload. I cry at baby commercials, I cry when I see a new baby. Often, I start crying out of the blue for no reason at all. I also feel fat, which doesn't help, and have no baby to show for it. I never know when the waves of grief will roll in.

Prayer and writing continue to give me strength during my darker times. Prayer reminds me that we are never alone and allows me to let go of my pain, if I choose to do so. As for my writing, I trust that if nothing else helps me, the divine messages that come through always offer insight, compassion, wisdom, and, most of all, a sense of peace. I write whenever the urge strikes. This is from today:

Your heart can dance to the music of life once again. With each new day, you can find strength in something that God has created, whether it be a sunrise or a butterfly. By looking at the beauty, you can be reminded of the power that is flowing to each and every person.

Sandy, with the passing of each day, you'll find that Talia's memories will continue to stay strong in your heart, but the ache that is there will eventually subside. She knew and still knows how deep your love is for her. You must take comfort in knowing that. There will be many days ahead when you feel you've taken a step backward on your road to healing. But know that you're on the healing path, which is paved with crevices to catch your tears. The tears that you shed will continue to cleanse you. Think of it as the water that feeds each beautiful rose along that healing path. Without your tears, the roses shrivel up and die. Don't let that happen to you emotionally. If you hold your feelings and tears in, you'll feel as though you want to withdraw from life.

Find a special place where you can be alone with Talia. It will help you keep your focus clear, and will help you to feel less overwhelmed in other areas. Take the time to experience what you're feeling. The solitude can help you to organize your thoughts and let you be in touch with your true emotions. You will be okay.

The tone of these messages strike me. The messages are consistently from a loving and wise perspective. I'm not sure of the source of this wisdom, but it isn't important to me. I feel as though I have a very wise, best friend that knows the depths of my soul and loves me unconditionally. What is important is that I keep connecting with it. These messages touch me at my very core. In the stillness of my soul, I know I will be okay.

August 5

Ariana's sleeping downstairs. We are having a bad thunderstorm this afternoon and we've just lost electricity. I'm in the bedroom and it's getting a little dark. The house is quiet. I want to take a nap, but I keep thinking about Talia and feel sad. Something is telling me that a message wants to be written. Here's what comes through:

> The tranquillity that is near you can be felt many different ways. You can relax your mind and body through meditation or simply through quiet time. Both are healing. It is during this quiet time that your inner resources can be maximized. That is to say, messages can come through more clearly.

> Tell others to slow down their pace of life. When one is so busy and detailed, it is impossible to center oneself to get a clear meaning of one's purpose — daily or long-term. You've been through that, and it isn't easy to break yourself away from that pattern. But once you do, you can find the

peace that has eluded you. While most people are searching far and wide for the answers to make them feel more secure, more happy, they may never find the answers that can easily be found by looking inward to their souls. Most will never understand that because they are too busy trying to put out fires caused by the distractions that, without realizing it, they themselves have caused.

Take time now to feel the peacefulness you've been waiting for, for so long. Be careful not to crowd your life again. There seemed not to be any room for another entity in your life. Do what makes you happy-whether it's playing with Ariana, writing, or just listening. It's healthy for your soul, and it is what you need at this point. The future has many possibilities for you. You are blessed with many talents. Keep yourself open to the possible changes that you may be guided towards as far as your work is concerned. Go with the flow of nature, and keep your heart open, and success can always be yours. Success should not be measured from the outside, but from the feelings within. The external forces that most people see can easily change. But the internal feelings are more stable and can benefit you more long term. They'll be with you longer.

Talia is busy, herself, helping other spirit guides. She is nudging you in her own gentle way. You may not feel it yet, but she is helping to give you a clearer direction for your life.

This message holds many truths for me. It's easy to see now, that in the past, a pattern had been established. I often kept myself busy in a subconscious effort to avoid dealing with things. That busyness then prevented me from being centered or focused, and then I would complain about how out of control I felt. I always thought busyness was a necessity not a choice.

"Success being measured from the feelings within…" also resonated within me. I've learned the hard way that success is more a sense of inner peace and love, rather than a job title or material wealth. How can I help people realize that they need to connect with their souls to find what they've been searching for? "Let it go…you don't need to know all the answers yet," I'm hearing in my heart. I live for these messages. Talia's death offered my soul the chance to live.

August 11

Another message:

> The first thing one must do on the road to recovery is to look at what really needs mending. Usually, the most obvious thorn points to some deeper issue. Some people try to get a quick fix. The pain goes away only temporarily but it comes from deep within one's soul. Once people are aware of that, they can open themselves to the healing force of nature and the universe on a more general level. For example, when one opens himself/herself to healing, love from others and from oneself can begin to permeate the deep layers of protective covering that have been built up over years.
>
> The inner core of one's self is pure and good. It is the effects from past hurts that change the purity. They alter the makeup of one's personality. But that core itself never changes — just the external layers do — whether they manifest in physical changes to a person's body or in emotional abnormalities. But again, a "clearing out" or "cleaning out" of the edges around one's soul can help the pure light to shine once again.

*You've cleansed yourself extensively through this last month
and a half. There are still tendencies to let external forces
block your most creative self, but take quiet time to reflect
on what's happening in your life. It can help you to keep the
mind-clutter away.*

I'm beginning to sense that these messages are stirring up
a reconnection to the wisdom of my core, my soul. The wisdom
has probably always been there, but I wasn't able to feel it until
I peeled off those external layers one by one.

I'm still not convinced from whom all the messages are
coming — God, a guardian angel, a spirit guide, or my own
highest self or soul, but it doesn't really matter to me. What
matters is that they are from a loving source. I am beginning to
understand that we are all connected at some deep level, all an
extension of God's spirit. I feel as if I'm a channel for this
wisdom — like a conduit. The writing is effortless on my part,
yet the wisdom is inspiring and insightful. Many of them don't
make total sense to me at first. The depth of the messages and
the words that come through aren't like my normal conversa-
tional language. I have to read and reread them, in order to
decipher the wisdom contained within.

August 12

It has been two and a half weeks since Talia died. Susie
came to pick up Ariana for a sleep over, so early this afternoon,
I was alone in the house. As a lion quietly and gradually sneaks
up on its prey before attack, intense sadness must have been
lingering around me, waiting for a quiet moment to pounce
upon me. And when it struck, it struck with full force. I hit rock

bottom. My thoughts were only of Talia and how much I missed her. Trying to dodge this pain, I frantically paced around the house, sobbing. I had to get my thoughts off Talia. Everywhere I looked there were reminders of her — pictures, new clothes, the rocking chair, her undisturbed crib. It was unbearable. I actually shouted out loud, "God, I need help!" About an hour later, Nancy (my sister) called and was concerned about how I sounded on the phone. She suggested that a walk might help. It couldn't hurt, so I headed out, with the intention of clearing my head. Bad idea.

As I walked, I realized how alone I felt in my sadness, and I began to cry. Mile one, two, I wasn't feeling better yet. In fact, the tears flowed harder. Mile three, almost home; I was an emotional wreck. About a quarter mile from home, a big tractor trailer approached. A fleeting, yet very disturbing thought went through my mind. In that moment, I really didn't care if that tractor trailer struck me head on. It would be an easy way to escape from the intense pain that followed me wherever I went. Luckily, the truck sped past me, and I had no choice but to head home. Part of me wants desperately to hold Talia again, and part of me is jealous that she must now know all the answers to life. My life seems bleak without her.

When I came back here to the house, I called Nancy and told her that I felt even worse than before. "No, I don't need you to come and visit. I'll be fine," I repeatedly told her. Truthfully though, I *was* terrified to be alone, fearful that these despondent feelings wouldn't go away. Nancy reminded me how peaceful I usually feel after I write. How could I so easily forget? I sat down on my bed, breathed deeply, and tried to quiet my emotions in an effort to receive a message that would help me.

The first word that I heard in my mind was "Mommy." Quickly dismissing what was surely too strange to write, I breathed more deeply. Relax. Let go, Sandy. The message will come. Over and over the same word persisted. "Mommy…Mommy…Mommy…," I kept hearing, so I wrote it.

This is what followed:

> Mommy,
>
> Please know that I'm okay. There is so much love here that I'm never alone. There is no suffering or heartache. You will see me again; although I'm not far from you now. My love is always surrounding you. Can you feel that peacefulness during times of great despair? That's us, taking care of you. Time is not relevant anymore, so don't think that it's going to be so long before we'll all be together again. I felt all the love from everyone at the hospital. Although I wasn't able to show it physically, I tried to give something back to each one of you. Remember the quiet times we had and cherish those times alone.

(The next part seemed to come from a more experienced spirit.)

> When the time is right for you, you'll be called to come back here. But until then, you must find the meaning of what is special in your life, and help others to find the same in their lives as well. There is nothing you can do to speed the process of life and learning. One lesson at a time; one experience will help you to build yourself for the next lesson. You are spiritually aware and can absorb much when you let yourself. Find the meaning within yourself — it's there that you'll find purpose for your life. Each event unfolds a map of unlimited opportunities. The path that you choose each day is up to you; however, the roads can be ever-changing. That is the challenge that helps people to grow and keep their spirits alive. If things were too predictable, people would find themselves at a loss for enrichment. That is how one's spirit dies inside.

At first I really thought I was losing my mind. How could this message have come from Talia? I have heard of mediums communicating with the dead, but I'm not a medium. Could this be real? I desperately want to believe that Talia really *could* feel all that love and that her spirit is still around us…but a letter from her? Despite all my doubt, my heart screams, "Believe it! Believe it! This writing is giving you evidence you can hold onto forever!" Tears of happiness and gratitude replace the sadness from the last few hours.

I called Nancy and read her what I just wrote. She was fascinated. Then, I called Rich at work. He didn't quite know what to think about all of this, since I can't *prove* it. But something in his voice sounded as though he believed it, too. Maybe, just maybe, he'll start to think differently. It doesn't matter what anyone else thinks; I know in my heart that Talia's spirit has spoken to me. Thank you, Talia, thank you, God, thank you, angels who are watching over me! I'm starting to feel like I am coming alive again. I now know that my mission in life is to help others find meaning in their own lives, to help them cut through all the layers of pain that may have accumulated over the years, and to help them realize that every experience has the ability to teach us something about life and about ourselves. This mission will give everlasting meaning to Talia's life. Through her life and death, this mission is born.

Twenty

It is now almost one month since Talia's death. My strength comes and goes without warning. There are still so many challenges to deal with. One that I'm confronting is how other people think I should be dealing with Talia's death. Recently, I was proudly showing some newly developed pictures of Talia to a relative. The shocked look in her eyes said more than her words ever could. That night, someone told me that she had suggested that perhaps I needed counseling, because I was showing pictures of Talia and still talking about her as though she's still with me. I believe that our willingness to talk about our loved ones who have died can help us in our healing process. And I do think she's still with me; I feel her in my heart. I hope I can *always* feel it.

It is also tough for me when I meet someone new and they ask the innocent question, "So, how many kids do you have?"

The first few times it happened, I replied, "Well, we have one at home, but…" and I'd go on to give the person a day-by-day rundown of all we had gone through with Talia.

I always sensed that I had shared too much, judging by the looks of horror on their faces. Once, I replied, "We have one," but then went home and cried because I felt so guilty over leaving Talia out. "One at home, and one in heaven," was my next approach. If they wanted to know more, I gladly obliged. That seems to feel right. I'm realizing that we are all different, and we must find what makes us feel the most comfortable. There is no right or wrong.

One of the toughest challenges, though, has been what to do with Talia's ashes. The funeral home called recently, suggesting I pick up her ashes when I felt ready. I was scared. I had no clue what her ashes would look like; I wasn't sure I'd be able to handle this. I was shocked when I arrived and the funeral director handed me a tiny, white box. This was it?

A couple of days later, when Ari was napping, I mustered up the courage to look inside the box. My hands were shaking as I slowly peeled the tape off the box. I had no idea what to expect. As I opened the box I felt weak, as if someone had knocked the wind out of me. Inside was a small, plastic bag containing what looked like a mixture of sand and crushed shells. Feeling nauseous, I immediately taped the box shut again. I quickly put it away with the rest of her memories; the sympathy cards, a lock of her hair, her hospital blanket, her ID bracelet. How could I be sure these were *Talia's* remains? I couldn't, except for the label on the outside of the box that had her name printed on it. I sat on my bedroom floor, stunned. Was this all that was left of Talia's life? It bears no resemblance to the memories of Talia that I have in my heart. I have to remember that her spirit will live on forever. What was inside that box was in fact the "shell" of her body.

I've been feeling frustrated because I feel the need for a special, designated place where I can grieve for Talia and talk to her. I can't bear the thought of getting a grave site for her, because I feel she'd be too lonely there. And what if we moved?

What would we do then? I can't dispose of her ashes yet. First of all, I feel that we have to find the *perfect* place to spread them, but, more importantly, I'm not ready to let them go. So I'm keeping them in my bedroom closet in a special box with her memories. At least she'll still be close to me, although I realize how odd that sounds.

Today I tried centering myself, writing down a question, then allowing the answer to come:

What should I do with the experience and pain of the last month? What is my next step?

> *The result of the events that have occurred will be shown in smaller ways than you had expected. Take the time to center yourself to hear the messages coming through to you. Once you do, you'll find the answers that you are looking for. You have not had the time yet to fully experience all the emotions that are necessary for growth. Do not jump too quickly into keeping yourself busy. When you do, you tend to ignore what is important for you to see at the moment. You are headed on the right track. You have made much progress in your spiritual journey. Focus on yourself first, then you'll be able to work your messages to help other people. Fully appreciate the opportunity for growth. You are among the chosen few.*

The connections that you feel with other people will be strengthened through our love. The new people that you meet will take on new importance. There are no chance meetings. In time, you will have prepared yourself for the ability to perceive what we are showing you through other people as well.

Will we have more children?

Again, you have been in preparation for what you are given. There will be others, when the time is right for you and for them as well. Patience is something that you have to work on. You have already realized that things will not always unfold on the timetable that you'd like. So shall it be with other spirits that will be born to you. They are here and are anxious to be in the physical world with you. There is an order to nature, although it is difficult for you to understand. It is not just you; but all who are in the physical form. On 9/29…one year….you will be enlightened once again.

We do feel more strongly connected with people lately. Perhaps there is an unspoken bond between those who have lost children. Shortly after Talia died, Rich and I attended a "HOPE" (Helping Other Parents Endure) meeting at South Shore Hospital in Weymouth. It was open to parents who had lost a child through miscarriage, stillbirth, or neonatal death. Since we fit two of the three categories, we were able to share quite a bit with other parents who had experienced similar losses.

Whenever I talked about Talia and how she has changed my outlook on life, I felt an electrical surge run through my body. I don't know if it's because she was around me at the time or because I feel so passionate about what I've been shown through my writing. I have a different perspective on life and death now, because of the messages. I realize not everyone shares the same outlook. We are all at different places along our journeys. I've learned that I have to respect where other people are on their own journeys, because everyone is different. Not better or worse, just different.

Some of the parents at the "HOPE" group had gone on to have other children. It was heartwarming to hear that life can indeed go on. Rich and I do want another child eventually. I just need a break emotionally and physically, after having had two miscarriages and then losing Talia. We are going to go along with the "natural order of nature," hoping that we'll sense when the time is right. If it is meant to be, it will be.

Twenty One

November 14

So much has happened in our lives in the last few months. In late August, Rich's company sent Rich, Ariana and me on a vacation to the destination of our choice. They wanted us to get away from everything and spend some quality time with each other. We picked Aruba, where Rich and I had honeymooned nine years earlier. We had always wanted to return. The vacation was exactly what we needed. The warm, crystal clear, blue ocean calmed our senses. The gentle breezes softened our brows. Ariana had such fun building sand castles and swimming. We felt as though there was some semblance of normalcy back in our lives. Guilt was never far away, though, and sometimes pierced through the happiness. "How can you dare to smile, laugh, and enjoy yourselves, when you so recently lost a daughter?" An ugly voice seemed to say. My soul responded, "Moving forward in life doesn't mean you've forgotten." I've realized that the voice of guilt is not usually our own, but comes from our fear of how others may be judging us.

When we got home from Aruba, I started a regimented exercise program. I was working out four or five times a week, trying desperately to find the shape I had once been in. My best friend, Karen, was an instructor at an aerobics studio about a half hour away. She invited me to take a class there. One day, on a whim, I decided I would go. On the way there, she casually mentioned that the owner was looking for a partner to invest in her business so she could remodel the studio. Her business had done quite well, and after a series of meetings with her, Rich and I bought into her business, becoming partners (talk about jumping right into the busyness again.) We, along with the original owner, were going to find a new location, invest in major renovations, and create a fitness center — a place where I could teach motivational workshops. It'd be a perfect combination, fitness for the body and mind.

I had some nagging doubts. Was I jumping in too quickly? Were we doing the right thing? Should I focus solely on teaching workshops and creating seminars? The new center wasn't going to be ready until February, so I had plenty of time to deal with all the doubts. Right now, I just want to get myself whole again.

Early in September, Rich and I decided to go for genetic counseling. We made an appointment with Dr. Murray Feingold, a well-known doctor who specializes in birth defects. We wanted to know if Talia's disorder could happen to us again. Dr. Feingold, a kind and gentle man, informed us that Talia's test results didn't point to any specific diagnosis. Without a clear diagnosis, there could be no definite determination on whether her condition was genetic. We had blood workup done anyway, with no notable findings. The unknown, with its uncertainty, lack of control, and twinges of discomfort, had become a permanent fixture in our lives. It also reminded me that during such times our best choice is to let go and let God. Furthermore, I didn't know if I was ready for any more kids yet, though I think it was because I was afraid to be emotionally vulnerable so soon.

It's funny how life often nudges us when it knows we're ready to move forward. I recently found out I am pregnant! I suspected it a few weeks ago, but two home pregnancy tests were negative. We were trying to take it one day at a time, with the understanding that if this pregnancy was meant to be, it would happen. Then, with the third home test, that beautiful blue line confirmed that I am pregnant. What a feeling of relief, as if I've finally done something right. We have mixed feelings of excitement and fear; we've decided that we aren't going to tell Ariana for a while.

"How can you not be worried? What if something happens again? Wow, Sandy, you're so brave." That's what one of my relatives said when I told her. I honestly don't consider myself brave. We are simply moving toward something that is important to us. We have no control over whether anything will happen to this pregnancy. If something does happen, we'll deal with it then. I know we'd make it through. Life goes on. I've come to understand that moving on in life doesn't mean that we've stopped loving our beloved ones who've died. It means that we've chosen to live. I've also learned in the last few months that if we put off living because of fear or grief, we slowly experience a more painful death, the death of our spirit.

I went for a routine ultrasound on the 26th of October. Based on my last period, I was probably seven weeks along, which would have made my conception date pretty close to that 9/29 date predicted in my writing. ("You'll be enlightened once again on 9/29.") The ultrasound technician said that the pregnancy sac appeared to be small, as if I were four or five weeks along. He also said he couldn't see a fetus in the sac. If I was seven weeks along, as I thought, he should be able to see something in the pregnancy sac by now. "It's too early to tell," he said, "but this pregnancy may not be viable and may terminate on its own. We'll just have to wait and see." Here we go again! Couldn't we just have a break? As we walked back through the waiting room, I looked around at the myriad of individuals waiting their turns for ultrasounds. I suddenly realized that there might be someone in that waiting room who was there for an ultrasound to check a potentially cancerous tumor. In an instant, I felt grateful that I was there because of a pregnancy and nothing more serious. Thank you, God, for reminding me once more. Everything turned out fine.

Also in October, I signed up for a two-day intensive journal writing workshop. Writing was becoming a more integral part of my life and this workshop was fabulous. It offered quiet time to reflect on all that has happened in my life. One of the questions in the workshop, "Where am I in the midst of my life?" evoked these thoughts:

> The death of our daughter, Talia, on July 24th, has made a profound impact on my life. Up until that point, I had certain beliefs about life and death, but that month she was alive exhaustively challenged everything I was made of. It could have knocked me down completely; however I feel entirely strengthened by her love. I feel more whole as a person. Rich, Ariana, and I shared an incredible bond, as did my whole family. I felt that I could trust everyone that I met. Since her death, I feel even more strongly that life is to be treasured, to be lived each moment. There can be such intense excitement in life, if we allow it to be.

> I am now staying at home with our daughter, Ariana. At first I felt that my talents weren't being used properly. I do feel that through the Dale Carnegie classes I teach and through talking with others, I can help them create better lives for themselves. I feel open to many new ideas, beliefs, and possible opportunities for my life. Although it took such sadness and pain just a few short months ago to bring me to where I am, I feel that this could be the most exciting and creative period of my life. I'm eating healthy and I'm dedicated to keeping (or rather, getting) myself physically fit. That makes me feel good.

Talia pried open the door to my spirituality. I've been getting incredibly meaningful messages through my writing, and I'm absolutely drawn to anything spiritual. Meditation classes, spirituality classes, spiritual books, and spiritual people are like magnets to my soul. Even the fact that I'm at this writing workshop tonight — I feel I was inspired by Talia to come here. I feel that because of her, the sunsets are more beautiful (or maybe I'm just noticing them now), the foliage is prettier, and music is more harmonious. I now have the time to enjoy peaceful sounds--the roar of the ocean waves, crickets chirping at night, the birds singing early in the morning.

What could have been devastating to my life has propelled me to a deeper understanding of who I am, shed light on my purpose in this lifetime, and awakened an appreciation of beauty around me. These are some of my blessings from Talia.

I need to rely more on my intuitive hunches and do what I want to do, rather than try to make everyone else happy. I need to be who I was destined to be and march to the beat of my own drummer. I think I've relied too heavily on other people's opinions for my life. No one can manifest my hopes and my dreams better than I, when I am guided by God's love and light.

Going to that workshop was one of the best decisions I've made! It's hard to describe the inner strength I feel after I write. Reflective journal writing encourages us to connect inwardly, allowing our internal flame to shine more brightly, which in turn sheds light on our life's purpose, our inner strengths, and our connection with a higher source of power.

Tonight, a few weeks after the workshop, I was feeling particularly restless around the house. I miss Talia, and I want to feel a stronger connection with her. It seems as if my pain is slowly fading, and I feel rather sad about it. Does this mean I am forgetting about her? Is it all right not to be in pain? I need to connect with her. I can't go to a cemetery and talk to her, because we still have her ashes here. I have an urge to write Talia a letter. I'm apprehensive at first, but I'll give in. I know I'll be dancing with my pain once again; what if I can't stop? Tears flow just as easily as these words flow from my pen.

Talia,

You would be just about four months old, if you were still with us here today. The first thought I get is that I know you're still here with us somehow, only not phys- ically. I often think about what you would look like, as I see Justin and Anthony (Karen and Christy's kids, born within a week of Talia) grow older. I know you'd be absolutely beautiful, my sweetheart. You are such a brave soul, making the choice to come into our lives, knowing that we'd have to go through such pain. You knew that we needed it in order for all of us to grow and develop spiritually. I admire you for being able to do that, Talia.

I remember how little you were when they first put you in my arms. You truly were our little "peanut". And you were so quiet. There was so much going on inside of you that no one knew at first. Ariana loved you right away, as did everyone who met you. Talia, I tried to protect you the best I knew how, and I loved you with all my heart. My heart ached for you every time you had another seizure, or every time your blood-oxygen level dropped. I wanted so badly to will all my strength and energy into you, and felt so frustrated and helpless when it didn't work.

You guided us through so many emotions and never did we believe that we'd be able to survive emotionally without you. But we are healing. Ariana talks about you all the time. She still includes you as part of our family, which you will *always* be.

We miss you Talia. Every time I go into your empty room, I feel a hollowness inside. It reminds me that I never got to rock you to sleep at home, or give you a bottle, or comfort you when you cried. I know that you felt our presence at the hospital, honey. I love you, Talia, and it makes me feel sad that I'll never get to hear those words from you, but I know that you loved us in order to do what you did. Thank you for being such a presence in our lives, Talia, and for the beautiful gifts you've given to us.

Love,

Mommy

I swore I heard, **"You're welcome, Mommy, I love you too."**

My tears are now running dry. I sense that I have cleansed more of my wounds. I wonder if our fear of getting lost in the depths of our pain prevents us from healing at our very core. I have learned that we can only heal what we can feel. If we only feel a little, we will only heal a little. So when we allow ourselves to face and feel our deepest pain, we pave the way for God's love and light to pour into our hearts, healing our deepest, darkest crevices, if we let it. Running from our pain only prolongs the process. Surrendering to it allows it to dissipate.

Twenty Two

With all the pain I had to experience, and with the specific messages that have come through my writing, telling me how to proceed with my life, one would think I'd have listened. Some people learn lessons quickly; perhaps I am a slow learner. It was certainly much easier for me to encourage *others* to listen to their hearts. I, on the other hand, had to be thumped on the head once again before I followed mine.

We opened the fitness center in February last year. Claire came to the grand opening. She was pregnant (due around the same time as me)! I was managing the fitness center a few days a week, bringing Ariana to work with me. It was wonderful at first. I didn't even care that I wasn't bringing a paycheck home. Since we were part owners, we had faith that the business would do well enough to start paying us a salary soon enough. I loved dealing with the public, and the clientele (mainly women) seemed like an extended family. Rich had kept his full-time job, and he worked at the fitness center a couple of nights a week. We spent Saturday mornings there, and I taught a meditation class on Sunday nights. But something wasn't right. Our family time was virtually nonexistent. And the interest level for the "mind" fitness wasn't there. Most people at our gym were far more interested in the aerobic and step classes. My soul was getting restless. "Sandy, this isn't for you," it gently whispered. I pretended not to hear it.

During the next year and a half in the business, I spent more and more time doing the administrative and managerial tasks, which was not my original intention. It was getting harder to ignore the stirring in my soul that told me that I wasn't in the highest and best place for me. My true purpose was to help people heal and grow emotionally and spiritually. At the fitness center, I felt I was at a dead end. My stress was on overload, and my family was feeling the brunt of it. We had lent the business a great deal of money, and it didn't seem as though we'd be able to turn a profit soon. Rich strongly suggested we hang in there until we at least recouped a portion of our losses. I, on the other hand, didn't want to wait. I wanted to be free but felt there was no way out. (There was, but I wasn't allowing myself to see my choices.) I felt stuck once again. Ugh! What a familiar feeling. Too often in my life, I've put off listening to my heart, because money or fear had a louder voice. I was disappointed in myself because I felt I should've known better. I've learned that lessons can repeat themselves. If we don't learn what we are supposed to learn from a situation or from a challenging person, the opportunity presents itself again, and again, until we learn. I'm hoping I got it this time — I'm tired of being stuck!

Finally, this summer, Rich and I sold our share of the business, walking away from a substantial amount of money. Though the financial loss was painful, the inner peace we felt over our decision was invaluable. The weight lifted from our shoulders was immense. I could easily look back at that period of my life as a major mistake, but I choose not to, for it taught me so many things. The most important lessons of that period were:

1. Listen to the callings of your soul. (Helloooo, have we not heard this one before??)

2. No amount of money is ever worth sacrificing your heart and soul.

3. You cannot put a price on your peace of mind.

Shortly after we got out of the fitness center, I began speaking to various groups and presenting workshops for companies, helping others to relieve the stress in their lives through meditation and a more positive attitude. But this fitness center chapter of my life has been an important one. It is a constant reminder to me that no matter how often we press the snooze button in life, what matters is that we finally choose to wake up.

Twenty Three

It has been nearly five years since Talia died. So many tears, so many lessons, so much growth on this journey of healing. I wonder if there ever is an end to life's healing process. Perhaps it is like the ocean, with its ebbs and tides. Sometimes the waves pound upon the shore, while others calmly and gently make their presence known. A sharp piece of glass on the beach will, over time, find its jagged edges polished into a beautiful, treasured piece of sea glass. So it can be with our hearts. As we give ourselves permission to fully feel the depths of our pain, we realize that over time, the emptiness lessens and the sharpness of our pain subsides. When we feel ready, we can choose to go on to live a life filled with joy; our loved ones who have died would support that. But no one can tell us when the time is right. It is a feeling from within.

When well-meaning individuals first heard of Talia's death, a common response was, "You're young, you'll have more children." I used to cringe. As if having another child would ever replace Talia. But I do admit that having Austin has further helped our hearts to heal. And the timing of his arrival couldn't have been more divine.

Rich, Ariana, and I were celebrating what would have been Talia's first birthday. After dinner, we had cupcakes and released pink balloons to the sky for her. Five hours later, I was in labor. And at 3:29AM, at Beth Israel Hospital, exactly *one year and one day* after Talia's birth, Austin Louis came bounding into the world! Same hospital, same doctors and nurses, another miracle of love. I imagined that Talia's spirit was there with us, helping Austin make his grand entrance. And when the doctor delivered him, I heard, "Congratulations…"

It's my brother!

Austin looked angry at the world when he was delivered. We didn't care, we were just so grateful that he was healthy. He has grown into a spunky little three year old, asserting his independence whenever he can. We are so thankful for him. Austin is a beautiful gift, who wouldn't be here today, had it not been for Talia. Having him come into our lives was like completing a circle that had been left unfinished. Having him at Beth Israel was like being able to tie a delicate bow around the most important chapter of our lives.

Austin has come to know Talia from pictures and from our conversations. Just recently he came out of his room holding one of his books.

"Mommy, I don't want this book anymore," he said. "I want to wrap it up and give it to Talia."

It took me by surprise, but I complied. "Okay, honey, we can, but how will she get it? She's in heaven."

"Mommy," he said matter of factly, "I just gonna wrap it up and put it behind the couch. She'll come down and get it and take it back with her."

I didn't quite know how I was going to see this through, but we wrapped up the book and put it behind the couch. An hour later, he changed his mind; he wanted to keep it after all. Phew! Things do have a way of working themselves out.

Austin recently said at the breakfast table, "Mommy, Talia's sitting right next to me. She told me she wants to watch Power Rangers with me." I don't doubt it. I'm sure that children can spiritually see and hear much more than we do as adults, simply because they haven't closed themselves down with fear. They're probably more receptive to a connection with the world of spirit because they're more open to it. I have found that we, too, can connect if we first believe it.

Ari used to make up stories about Talia. When she was almost four, she proceeded to tell me a story about her. I grabbed a pen and recorded it on a napkin:

"Talia is a special angel. She has special wings. She can fly up with her special wings. If she falls down, she can fly up again. But if she breaks her head, Claire can fix her again. If she misses her family, she can fly down from the sky that's blue. If she breaks her toes, she can glue them on. Claire can glue them on again. But if she breaks her whole bone off, she has to break her whole self off, and God will fix her. If God falls down, Talia flies up again. If Claire falls down again, she'll break her whole body off.

Daddy is so special — he can cook, run and watch baseball. He loves football and baseball games. And also soccer and also golf. And if he falls down and breaks his head, he will fall down and break his whole body. Mommy is so special to fly him up. And Austin is so special because he's got wings too. Our whole family has wings because they're so special. If they fall down without their hands behind their backs, then they will break their whole body. And I'm so special — I can be a whole special girl."

Ari *is* a special girl. She makes me laugh when I need it the most. They both do.

I recently asked Ariana, now seven, what she remembers about Talia. This was her response.

"I remember that I gave her that gray dinosaur, and she had tubes in her nose. She had a black thing on her belly (her bellybutton). I remember I loved her. I got to hold her in the rocking chair. Oh yeah, and she threw up on Nana. I wish Talia would come back. I'm imagining that she would be four now, and that I would have a lot of fun with her, but she's in heaven."

Then I asked, "What do you think heaven is like, Ari?"

"It's cloudy, but it never rains up there. The clouds must make a really good bed, and you wouldn't need pillows. God takes care of the angels, and the angels watch over us."

I couldn't imagine it better.

Ariana often talks openly about Talia. She includes her little sister in our family count. If anyone asks her if she has any brothers or sisters, she proudly replies, "Yes, I have a little brother Austin, and a baby sister, Talia, who's up in heaven." When drawing pictures of our family at school, Ari frequently draws Talia in the picture as an angel. It warms my heart. I learn so much from Ariana and how she easily speaks what she feels, not worrying about what others will say. As much as we're supposed to be teaching our children, I firmly believe our children have as much, if not more, to teach us.

As we continued to heal, we reached a milestone on our healing journey — letting go of Talia's ashes. Rich and I planned a return trip to Aruba last spring, with Ariana and Austin. A few weeks before we left, I sensed that the time seemed right to spread her remains. Our hearts had healed so much. And Aruba had always had special meaning for us. Rich agreed. The crystal clear waters would be a beautiful setting. I envisioned a picture-perfect moment, as Rich and I, teary-eyed, lovingly spread Talia's remains, while Ari and Austin played unknowingly near-by. The reality couldn't have been further from that image.

The night before we left Aruba to come back home, we brought the box with us to dinner. We planned to have a little ceremony afterwards on the beach. It was a beautiful night. The moon was nearly full; the wind gently played with our hair. The candlelight dinner outside set a perfect mood for what we had planned afterwards. Well, almost. By the time we got to the beach, it was around 9:30PM. Austin had been having tantrums ever since dinner because he was tired (a mother's favorite excuse!). Ariana had to go to the bathroom so badly that she had a partial accident in her clothes before we could find her a bathroom. They sat on a lounge chair nearby, oblivious to the importance of this night. The winds seemed to change, angrily tossing up loose sand that began to hit our faces and made Austin cry even harder! I tried to savor the moment, but Rich was getting frustrated. He said, in a tone that didn't hide his mood, "Can we *please* just get this over with now?" So much for the Kodak moment.

I took the bag with Talia's remains out of my pocket as Rich and I headed towards the water. I went first. I gently tossed a handful of ashes, which felt more like coarse sand, into the sea. As it landed upon the surface, the water seemed to sparkle magically like diamonds in the moonlight. Aah, this was what I had pictured. "I love you Talia!" I whispered into the darkness, waiting to be overcome by emotion. For some reason, it never came. Ariana heard me, and she asked what I was doing. Rich wondered if we should have Ariana help us with this ritual. "No!" I exclaimed. How could we explain to her that these were her sister's remains we were throwing into the water? We told her it was magic dust we were throwing into the sea for good luck. Luckily, she was too tired to ask any more questions. When it was Rich's turn, he said, "Good-bye, Talia, we love you, and we'll come back and see you again." Oh my God, I was horrified! "Rich, honey, we're not really leaving Talia here in Aruba; her spirit will always be near us." He nodded, then took another handful. As he was about to toss it into the ocean, a big gust of wind swept most of it back into our faces, the small particles scratching our eyes. As I reflect on that night, I have a smile in my heart from all the things that went wrong. It was not at all as I'd envisioned, but perhaps it was the way it was meant to be.

Twenty Four

My work has taken on greater meaning and purpose since Talia died. A year after Austin was born, I created LifeCraft, whose mission is to offer workshops that help individuals look within, reconnect to their core, to God's love and light, and move toward their dreams. It hasn't been without challenges; however, I realize now they were self-imposed challenges. It took me about a year to build the courage to speak about my spirituality even though it had become an integral part of my life. Initially, most of the workshops were on building morale and stress management in the corporate world. The way I kept myself motivated and dealt with stress was through reconnecting with my soul, praying, and letting it go to God. However, I never allowed myself to say that in a public forum! My fear was that somehow I wouldn't fit in if I spoke about a higher power, the soul, and especially the G-word (God). "People aren't ready for this, they'll reject you, it's not appropriate, " my fear would caution me. Therefore, I felt a sense of incongruence between what I believed and what I taught. My fear trapped me, but God offered me an opportunity to break free from those traps.

In August of 1997, I was presenting a series of workshops to homeless veterans living at a shelter in Boston. The workshops were on self-esteem, stress management, and conflict management. Attendance at these workshops was mandatory. Needless to say, many of those 50 or 60 men were not happy about having to be there, and made no attempt to hide it.

This particular day, I had taken the subway into Boston and arrived with time to spare. It was only 5:30 p.m.; my workshop didn't start until 6:00. I usually drove in, and most times found myself rushing to get there on time, since traffic through Boston is often slow and very unpredictable. It had been a beautiful, sunny day. A nearby park bench beckoned me to rest. The sun warmed my face as I closed my eyes and began to pray for the group, as I normally do before my presentations. "God, please speak through me tonight. Help me find the right words that will reach their hearts. Thank you for this opportunity to touch their lives in some way." Suddenly, I got a strong urge to write. I quickly grabbed my pen and notepad. With my eyes partially blurred, the following powerful message came flowing from my pen:

8/19/97

Sandy, give my love to them, and let them know that I'm always here for them, whether they call upon me or not. Tell them to choose love, to choose peace, to first and foremost love themselves unconditionally. If they can leave the hurts and the frustrations in my hands, I can heal their wounds. To ignore their own pain is to push it down even further.

This is why you're there, Sandy, to open their eyes to the fact that I never left them--they chose to leave me. Even in the depths of their innermost pain, I was there, waiting to be called upon. Some may reject these words tonight altogether, and that's okay — the thoughts will remain with them for a later point in their lives. There are some, however, whose hearts have been aching to hear these words, and you are my messenger.

*Their spirits are, were, and always will be pure and loving.
It is merely the cobwebs in their outermost layers that
prohibit them from feeling this. Many have expressed so
vividly the inner turmoil and pain that has been their
experience for so long. To try and work through it alone is
to try and sort through the muck and mire in the midst of
darkness. I am the light that they need.*

After I read what was written on the page, I felt chills. Was I really supposed to share the message with them? I strongly sensed that I needed to read it to them, but my fear taunted me. "They're going to laugh at you. They're not going to be open to the message. Many of them are angry at the world. The workshop is about conflict resolution and you're going to read them a message about God's love?" My soul urged me to do it. I've learned that the voice of fear is loud; the voice of the soul is persistent.

The workshop wasn't one of the best ones I'd done. A few of the men were talking to each other in the back of the room the entire time; one man was paying his bills right in the front row; another read a newspaper. It was hard to stay focused. At the end of the presentation, though, I still sensed a need to read them the message. I breathed deeply, summoned my courage, and took a chance. I prefaced it by explaining what had happened on that park bench, then said, "There may be at least one person here tonight who may benefit from this message. I'm not sure why, but I feel compelled to share it with you." Then I read it. Some understood the message right away and came up and hugged me. A few looked perplexed, as though it might take more time to sink in, and many looked as though they didn't *ever* want to get it!

Riding home on the subway that night, I was filled with joy. It was the same feeling I had the day of Talia's memorial service, after I read her tribute. I felt that, once again, God had nudged me to do something way out of my comfort zone, and I responded. In those moments, my need for approval doesn't exist. I've learned four things from that night.

1. Our job is to spread seeds. We are not responsible if others do not choose to let them grow.

2. We don't need to save the world all at once. In fact, we don't need to *save* anyone at all. If we can make a positive difference even in just one life, we'll have made an impact on the world.

3. When we respond to God's gentle nudgings, we open ourselves to receive unconditional love.

4. We must be true to who we are.

Since I have come out of my spiritual closet and have become more clear about who I am, I have found that my work has shifted. I have been blessed with the right audiences for me. My workshops and seminars now help people believe in themselves once again, listen for the voices of their souls, and reconnect with their spirituality. When we have courage to step out and stand behind the truth of who we are, God and the universe will support us in many ways, and nudge us, moving us in new directions for our life.

I'm learning to trust those gentle nudgings, knowing that they will place me on the highest path for my life. Since last year, I've felt a strong pull to learn more about the world of spirit. It started with a vision, then was reinforced by a dream. Late one night almost a year ago, I was in that in-between pre-dream state, and I had a vision of a little girl who was in spirit. My eyes were closed, but it was crystal clear. She appeared to be about four or five years old, with light brown curly hair. I was shocked to see her! This had never happened to me before. I wasn't quite sure what to say.

"Hi there. Who are you?" I asked her.

"My name is Rachel. You've got to help me find my Mommy. You've got to tell her I'm okay."

"I don't know who your Mommy is."

"You've got to help me find her and tell her I'm okay," she repeated.

I didn't recognize this small child, but reassured her, that I would tell her mother that she is okay. That vision, that lasted for a minute, has haunted me since then. She seemed so desperate to find a way to get through to her mommy. I pray and trust that I will meet her mother when I am supposed to.

Then there was that vivid dream last year. In it, I was speaking to a group of individuals in a dark bookstore or a library perhaps. I don't remember the topic, but I started speaking about losing a child. As I spoke, more and more people filled the room, all of whom were parents who had lost a child. I could actually see the spirits of their children right behind them! I was able to communicate with them, bringing their parents messages of love and hope. That dream has played itself repeatedly in my mind. I sensed it was more than just a dream — it felt like a sign to me that someday I'd be able to connect with spirits that have left this earth plane.

Since February of this year, I have been taking weekly classes in mediumship, to strengthen my link to the spirit world. I've learned how to link with people in spirit and bring back their loving messages for friends and family. Many people are afraid of mediumship, imagining seances with ghosts flying around and making objects move, or spirits taking over your body. It is nothing like that. I'm finding this work to be filled with love, bringing healing into people's hearts. And none of this would have happened without the gift of Talia.

Another gift from Talia has been the reconnection to the divine messages coming through my writing. They have shed light on challenges, given me insights into my soul, and confirmed that there is a loving presence all around us. When I settle myself down to connect with the Source of this wisdom, it never fails to be there. I write when I feel grateful and joyous, and the messages offer confirmation that I'm on the right path. I also write when I'm confused, angry, or overwhelmed, and the messages offer love and healing.

One such message came in September of 1997. Princess Diana had died in a tragic car accident on August 31. Her death stunned the world. A few days later, Mother Teresa died, causing even more grief to an already devastated world. And the very next day tragedy struck closer to home. My brother-in-law's nephew, Jimmy Castagnozzi, Jr., 27, died when the plane he was piloting crashed in Rhode Island. As I often do when I feel overwhelmed with emotion, I sat down to write. This particular day, I wrote a question for God:

9/7/97

There is such turmoil all around us, God — first the death of Princess Diana, then Mother Teresa, and now Jimmy. Such loss and sadness. What can we do with all of this? How can I help people heal through this? (The following response came immediately.)

Send them love, Sandy, whoever is in your path of vision (both internal and external). Don't turn away just because it may involve tears on your part. All the more reason to be there.

*The sadness is like a cloud cover-it feels heavy, and people actually feel a heavier burden on their shoulders. When there is nothing but gray skies, as people see it, they cannot see beyond it. But a part of them **absolutely** knows that there is sun there at all times; it just cannot be seen. Such is the light from my love. It is there all the time, but many choose not to see or feel it. As soon as they get to the point in their lives where they are willing to let me into their hearts, I can help them heal their hurts. I have the power to move the clouds away. The light shall shine through to them.*

*You need to tell them this message. It may not sink in, but it will rest within their hearts, until they are ready for it. At this point, they may need to **feel** the pain, to feel the sadness and process that. You are to offer hope and healing beyond their pain. You worked through your pain with my help. Let them know that I also am waiting to help them. Their hearts need to know this.*

It may not seem fair at all that life will go on around them, but it does. The sun will rise, the sun will set, the leaves will fall and return again in the spring. The message to this is that there is life once again — even after a tragic loss. Seeds of hope need to be planted.

I felt peace in my heart. But the phrase "seeds of hope need to be planted" played over and over again in my mind. I sensed that there was an important message there for me to act upon, but it wasn't clear to me. A few days later, it all made sense! I reflected on all the divinely inspired writing I had done since Talia had died. The "seeds" were the powerful insights and words of wisdom from the writing that came through me. Their messages had given me inner strength and inspiration on my journey. I sensed this message was telling me it was now time to share them with others. I needed to look for those seeds — they were waiting to be sown!

In the spring of 1998, the Seeds of Hope™ collection was born — inspirational pocket cards whose messages help individuals find hope, strength, courage, and insight on their own journeys. Once again, a lesson emerged. The pieces to our life's puzzle are all around us. We simply need to be open to them, and take action when we find them.

Receiving divine guidance is easier than most think, but doesn't have to come in the form of writing. It is all around us, waiting to be recognized. It can come to us through a whisper in our souls — "Love yourself, slow down and appreciate life, follow your dreams, let love into your heart." Yet how often do we not trust that still, small voice? Sometimes the prodding comes to us in the words of a song on the radio, in our dreams, from the mouths of our children, or even on a billboard on the highway. We are often too busy, however, to notice the signs. The answers for our life can be presented through wonderful coincidences, yet we don't always see the connection, dismissing them as silly events. Perhaps we are looking for God to manifest a lightning bolt along with the answer. If we saw it, we'd probably doubt its validity. Sometimes, though, the signs can be very obvious.

In November of 1997, I was to present my first public seminar entitled, "The Spiritual Path to Success." Two months before, I had been praying for guidance during the preparation stage. "God, help me deliver the right message for this audience," I prayed. One Friday afternoon, I had gone grocery shopping with Ari and Austin. We were on our way home, and Ari repeatedly asked if we could go to Blockbuster Video to rent a movie. We had no plans for the night, so I turned the car around, and headed back to Blockbuster, which was right next to the super-market. I pulled into the parking lot, and the movie "Michael," with John Travolta as an archangel, came into my mind. Friends had been raving about it. I wanted to see it, especially because I had recently had a dream about an angel named Michael, who told me that he was going to help me with my writing. Maybe there was a connection. But I was only planning to get a movie for each of the kids. Maybe I'd rent "Michael" another time.

We walked into Blockbuster. I immediately had shivers up and down my spine! I looked up at the three TV monitors hanging from the ceiling. There was *John Travolta* on the screen! It wasn't the movie "Michael" playing though, it was the movie "Grease." Incredibly, just as we moved closer, he began singing, "Sandy, can't you see…" I wanted to scream, "Yes, I can see, I can see! I'll get the movie!" I did rent "Michael" that night and loved it. And there was a connection. The main theme of the movie was: All you need is love; love is all there is. That became one of the messages for my seminar.

That message was presented to me in a different way a few weeks later. I was still praying for guidance on the seminar. Rich and I and the kids were visiting his mom and her husband in Connecticut. We were spending the night there; the four of us in the same room. At 2AM, Ariana woke me up and asked if I would take her to the bathroom. When we got back, Rich and Austin were snoring, and Ariana soon joined in with this "nasal symphony." I couldn't sleep! I lay there for a short while, then decided to meditate, in an effort to help me relax and block out the snoring.

I did become more relaxed, but started feeling myself being lifted up off the bed, leaving my body behind. Traveling up, up, up, I could see that there was a whitish/silvery cord attached to me. The other end was attached to the most magnificent white/golden light (similar to the one I'd seen many years ago). I sensed it was God, because the pure love emanating from this light was overwhelmingly powerful and bright. I couldn't look directly into the light. As I got closer to this light, it "spoke" to me through my thoughts. As it sent a thought to me, a painful surge of electricity ran through my body. This happened five or six times. I don't remember what those thoughts were, but I do remember the following words spoken in my left ear so loudly and clearly, "Tell them to leave the past behind and return to Me." I must have gotten scared, because as quickly as it began, I was jolted back into my body with a thump and fell asleep shortly thereafter. And I was left with an important message that was imprinted on my heart.

The next day I told Rich about my experience. "Uh huh," was his response. Though he doesn't have the same experiences, nothing really surprises him anymore. He may not always understand what happens with me, but he listens to my stories. I sense that on some level he's beginning to see the correlation of events around *him*. I've learned that I cannot force anyone to see what I see, or to believe what I believe. I honor and respect others' opinions and views about God, for I realize that my beliefs may not feel right to another. My place is not to judge what's right for another; it is to share my experience and to offer love and acceptance. We are all on our own journeys. God and my soul are my tour guides.

Twenty Five

My understanding of God has evolved and been strengthened through the years. God, to me, is the essence of life, the life force that connects you and me. I feel God is the universal Spirit of light that is present in and around us. God offers unconditional love, is at the heart of our creativity, and urges us to re-create ourselves anew. At any time, you can tap into this powerful source of strength and love. You no longer have to walk your path alone. If you want your pain to cease, for your path to be more well-lit, you can choose to feel God's powerful presence in your life. God waits to help you and guide you.

Perhaps you are like I was. I couldn't sense God's guidance around me, therefore it didn't exist. Looking back, I realize that my fear got in the way. If I opened my soul to God and nothing happened, I'd have been left raw and exposed. That fear was a far cry from reality. Yet still I struggled on my own. I imagine that the scenario is similar to the scene of our son Austin getting dressed when he was about two years old. He tried so hard, yet he could only go so far. Somehow, he always managed to get his arm through the neck hole, and his head stuck in the arm hole!

"Austin, can I help you, honey?"

"No, Mommy, I do it myself!"

As his frustration mounted, so did his resolve. Repeated attempts to help him brought only more stubbornness. I'd wait outside his room until he realized, at last, that he couldn't do it alone. Exhausted and worn, he'd finally call out, "Mommy, can you help me?" If I had forced him before he was ready, he would have resisted. When he was ready to let go, he gratefully accepted my help. Before we let go of our own ego barriers, we, too, may feel as if life is a struggle. Sometimes, because of our pain or fears, we close our hearts to God, to the Source, to the abundant flow of love, to our soul.

When this soul connection is lost, we end up living our lives from our ego. Our ego's view of the potentiality of who we are is not the highest view. It is based not in love, but in fear, hurt, and pain. We may often sabotage our best efforts because this ego, the inner critic, is telling us, "That's far enough, you'll never get past this, you've never done it before, who are you to deserve this." That inner critic occasionally peeks out through the layers of fear, but is deeply hidden. Its voice is so loud because it desperately wants to be heard. When we listen to its caustic voice, we limit ourselves in our thoughts, our words, and our actions.

Perhaps you have lived with that negative voice as your guide through life for far too long. Consider how different the voice of the ego sounds compared with the loving voice of the soul.

The ego says:	The soul says:
You need to be perfect.	You are perfect in this moment.
You have to be right.	Do the right thing.
What if…	So what…
It's just a silly coincidence.	Coincidences are guideposts.
Show me the money!	Feel the passion.
Ignore your fear — it'll go away.	Face your fear — it will dissolve.
Don't risk a broken heart.	Love is worth the risk.
Be like everyone else.	Be who you are.
Follow the path that you know.	Follow your heart.

If only we would reconnect with our souls. We can at any time. When we listen to our souls, we become one with the natural flow of life. We become one with God. Our lives become smoother. Little miracles abound, and coincidences are everywhere. They are like guideposts, pointing us in the right direction at the right time. When I am connected to my soul, I have patience with my children, my creativity flourishes, and all seems right with the world. When I get carried away with the busyness of life, I feel out of control and stressed, and I see the challenges rather than the gems.

It matters not how many times we subconsciously disconnect from our soul, what matters is that we connect once again. Our biggest challenge in life is first to *remember* that our core is pure love and light. Then reconnect however possible. For me, it is through prayer, meditation, and writing.

Prayer is an important part of my life. I pray in my car, in the shower, wherever and whenever the mood strikes. Prayer reminds me that I am not alone, and that I can draw strength whenever I need it. And it can be a much-needed reminder to offer gratitude for the abundance of blessings already in my life. When I have a spirit of gratitude, I often find more things for which I am grateful.

Meditation is also a powerful tool. It quiets the mind chatter and encourages a return to our spiritual core. I have been meditating for years now and run meditation classes in the sun room we had built when Talia was born. It has a special energy there. Through meditation I have connected with many spiritual guides and angels who are helping me on this journey. We all have these guides and angels. They, too, are waiting to offer wisdom and guidance to ease our travels.

As far as writing, I use this simple, three part process to connect with God, my angels, my soul:

1. Ask: This first step is to humble yourself to the fact that you do not know all the answers. Once I admitted to this, I was able to release pressure I'd put on myself for years. I like not knowing all the answers — it opens me up to finding better solutions to my challenges! Find a quiet place, where you can quiet your mind chatter. Put on some relaxing music, if you prefer. Take a few deep, cleansing breaths, then write out your question. Sometimes if I don't have a burning question, I'll simply write, "What do I need to know at this point in my life?"

2. Listen: This step is even more important. Many times we keep asking God questions, and never quiet down long enough to hear the responses! Sit and wait, until your pen wants to record a thought. Detach from the thoughts, as if they are coming to you, not from you. Allow the stream of thoughts to flow. Write whatever words or images you get. Try not to judge or censor what's coming through. If it sounds or feels negative, it's probably coming from your fear, and not from a higher source. Let go, and allow the loving thoughts to come through.

3. Act: This has traditionally been the hardest step for many — to take action based on the loving advice that you get! But please trust it. It will always lead you to where you need to be at this moment.

When you open yourself to divine guidance in your life, you will hear the answers that you need to hear, not necessarily the ones you *want* to hear. I don't believe I'm singled out to receive messages from God. I believe that we *all* have that ability, and we can choose to experience it at any time.

Twenty Six

As I continue to receive information from my guides, it makes life seem almost simple. We're the ones who make it so difficult. Within each of you is your soul, the innermost loving part of who you are. It is the place of your highest truth, wisdom, love and beauty. Your soul is where God can speak to you in the most intimate of ways. The purpose of your core of light is to shine brightly, illuminating your worth and shining a light on the gifts within all experiences.

You travel through the valleys of life's challenges and hurts, however, and sometimes create walls, filled with unexpressed emotions. Those outer musty layers keep the soul from fully manifesting itself in all its glory. The accumulation of layers also prevents the world from seeing the true beauty of who you are, a spiritual being of love.

However, your soul continually whispers to you, in an effort to guide you here, nudge you there. If only you would heed its gentle calls.

In an unexpected vulnerable moment, the light from your soul peeks through the tiny cracks in your walls. You sense a shift. You sense that there is wonder and beauty and love within you that longs to be expressed. It becomes painful to maintain those walls, and you make a choice to remove those stubborn layers, one by one, with the intense desire to reconnect to that love, that light, that beauty within you. As you choose to experience the *feeling* of each heavy layer, it is no longer needed for protection. As each layer is removed, you open yourself spiritually. Reconnection to one's soul is not always an easy path to choose, but it is one well worth the effort.

Once you reconnect, you can see the power of your choices, thoughts, and intentions. Once you reconnect, you can hear God's still, small voice of love, and connect with the divine love and light within you. Once you reconnect, you can shift your consciousness from fear to love. You learn how to rebuild trust in yourself, and take action based on your inner wisdom and guidance. Once you reconnect, when you ask for divine guidance to help you through your challenges, you can see, hear, and sense the answers that are being given to you. The people who then cross your path are often messengers for God, and offer you a clue to the puzzle of life. Once you reconnect, your soul can dance once again in the fullness of its light.

Final Reflection

As I was out taking a walk this morning, I approached a yard that sported a very large tree with incredibly vibrant red leaves, many of which were on the ground. How sad that seemed. What a waste of their beauty! Countless cars sped by this sight every day. Did anyone notice or care? I wanted to scoop up a handful of these fallen leaves and surround myself with their beauty and aroma. I thought about ringing the doorbell of that tree's owner, asking if I could take a bunch of the leaves home with me. What an odd request to make. Fearing I'd be laughed at, I didn't do it.

A mighty tree in our own backyard also has leaves of breath-taking beauty — a brilliant shade of red. This fall morning, I notice that most of its leaves have also made their descent, gracing the cool ground. I feel saddened for the tree, which has had to part with its own offspring. I am reminded of Talia. I feel moved to write a letter to this tree, which to me, symbolizes any parent who has suffered the loss of a child.

"I feel so badly that something so beautiful, so vibrant has to be separated from you. Some of your leaves are blown far away, some are quite content to hang around for a bit longer, and others are gently picked up by loving hands, eager to preserve their beauty for all of eternity."

The tree seems to respond, *"Although I start out with green leaves, it takes some time for them to mature and reach their peak color. Once they do, they are ready to move on. Does it make me sad? No, because I know they've left their little marks not just on my branches, but they've added beauty to others' lives as well."*

"But don't you want to cling to them, so you'll be protected by their warmth?" I asked.

Calmly, the mother tree continues, "I *have inner warmth and security that I rely on when they're not here. And no, I don't cling to them. Not because I don't want to, but because I cannot as a law of nature. To go against that would be to go against the natural order of the universe. I have come to learn, in all my mature years, that their beauty never leaves me. Their physical form may not be here, but they are here in spirit. They are all on their designated paths.*

Feeling more panic, I say, "I still find it so hard to let go of things that I love and treasure. I find that I can share them for a little while, as long as I know that they're coming home. Otherwise, it's much too painful to say good-bye."

The wise old tree lovingly answered, "*There are never really any permanent good-byes at all. Life never does end; it just takes on new form. After a period of parting, there may be a brief period of barrenness, in which you feel that all your life is gone. But new life will emerge in the spring once again, of that you can be sure. You have my word.*"

Once again, there was a life lesson right in front of my eyes.

"Thank you, Mother Tree."

"*You're welcome.*"

Thoughts from Rich...

When Talia was born, she looked like a little porcelain angel. Physically, she looked perfect. So when they told us that there could be something wrong with her, I knew they were wrong. I refused to believe Talia was anything but perfect. I realize now I was in denial. I knew there was no better hospital for Talia to be in, but I just knew everybody was wrong about her. I was so afraid of losing her. As time went on, I felt angry, because of her unknown future. I kept all this in, because I felt like I had to be strong for Sandy's sake. Not that she was weak, by any means, but I felt that if I crumbled, I couldn't be there for her. I have never told this to anyone, but part of me felt somewhat responsible for Talia's illness. Perhaps it was something genetic that I had passed on to her.

I know Sandy felt more connected with God during this time. But I wasn't even thinking about God. I was more interested in finding the scientific cause of Talia's sickness. I wanted answers. Spirituality never entered my mind. And prayer was not a part of my life. I didn't even know *how* to do it, although I never felt as though anything was missing from my life from lack of prayer.

In the very beginning of her stay at the NICU, I distanced myself from Talia on purpose. I didn't want to hold her at first. I thought that if I didn't get too attached, I wouldn't have to hurt so much. I didn't want to set myself up for a fall. Then, the day I decided to hold her on my chest, with all her tubes, nothing else mattered. I decided I was going to enjoy every moment we had with her, rather than worry about my heart breaking.

One of the ways I coped with all the uncertainty was going back to work. I was the controller for D'Angelo's sub shops at the time. I needed some normalcy, and thought that work could offer that to me. Perhaps if I went to work, and got away from it all, I'd feel normal again. While I'm sure it was unintentional, I found that many co-workers treated me as though I had some type of disease. No one seemed to want to come into my office, whereas on an average day, at least 50 people with questions would visit. I'm sure they didn't know what to say, or how to react. And I felt I was making them uncomfortable, just by being there. But I still kept going to work a few days a week, because my office was a place where I could escape, and return to where my life had been before we found out about Talia's problems. I never told Sandy (until now) about the times I was by myself (often when I was driving home), when the feelings of anger, sadness and frustration were so overwhelming that I'd cry in the privacy of my car.

I was never one to openly discuss my feelings easily. I just never did that while I was growing up. If I had a problem, I'd handle it on my own. When my father was diagnosed with cancer in the mid-1980's, I couldn't cry for the longest time. I was living in Massachusetts, and my parents were in Connecticut. As his disease progressed, I tried hard to remember him as the healthy, fun-loving father I once knew. Then one night, we went to a testimonial dinner that the Board of Education had for him. I hadn't seen him in a couple months. He looked horribly drawn, and he was in a wheelchair. This was not the father I remembered. I cried long and hard that night, because the truth was slowly sinking in that my father was going to die. When he died in April of 1986, he was 54 years old, and very close to retirement. When I was younger, I had heard him talk about special trips he and my mother would take — after he retired. So, through his death, I learned an invaluable lesson: Life is too short. Live in the moment.

Over the years, I'd forgotten that lesson. I got caught up in the hectic pace of life and wrapped up in my career. Losing Talia forced me to stop and once again appreciate what I did have in my life outside of work — Sandy, Ariana, and now Austin. Life is so precious, yet we often take so much for granted. This realization was the gift Talia gave to me.

Epilogue

Thank you for allowing me to share a very intimate part of my life with you, my kindred spirits. As I wrote this book and relived many of the moments, there were tears shed — more healing I suppose. A few days after Talia started having seizures, I'd always sensed I'd be writing a book about her. In fact, that vision I had almost five years ago of being on Oprah with Talia, my miracle child, included Oprah holding a book saying, "So this is the book you wrote about your daughter..."

I knew someday this book would become a reality; it was just a matter of the right timing. A message through my writing back in November of 1994 has continually given me the encouragement to finish the book.

11/4/94

Sandy,

When one "life" ends, another can begin. Where one seedling sprouts, the dirt must make way for this new growth. The cocoon is but an empty shell from where the beautiful butterfly is able to spread its wings. There IS a purposeful flow to nature, and the environment, but it applies to human life as well. The pieces of the puzzle don't always seem to make sense as you're putting them together one by one, but the picture is much different once a section is completed. Sometimes you must look at it from a higher perspective in order for it to make sense. Many people just find themselves occupied with the "doing," and don't have time for the "being." You have fallen into that trap on many occasions, but luckily, we're able to send a particular message that will get your attention.

The process wasn't completed before, that is why Talia's spirit could not stay. But it was not your fault at all for not being ready. She helped you align yourself for your writing to happen, and for your dedication to get messages out to others. You were doing well at it before, but we needed you to step up the intensity, and she wanted to help you out. She is a beautiful spirit. Write about her…about your feelings and emotions you've all been through…not just from your perspective, but from those in your family, and Rich's as well. This can help many others to cope, and to help their loved ones cope with a loss. Take the time to do it, Sandy, the world is waiting to hear about it.

So here it is, my gift to you. I hope that you've been able to gain strength from the lessons I've learned from Talia's life and death.

There is no more pain today when I talk about Talia's lessons, as I sometimes do in my speaking engagements. It amazes me how many people approach me after a talk, speaking of miscarriages or the loss of a child or of someone they know who had suffered such a loss. Loss hits us all at some point. Our willingness to talk about our experiences can help others face their own challenges and gain courage, to continue along their journey of spiritual healing.

There is a common thread to each painful life challenge, whether it is a loss of a child, spouse, parent, sibling or any other loved one, or a "death" of another kind — a divorce, separation, layoff. Each experience offers you the opportunity to see the precious gems hidden beneath the pain, to reconnect with God, and to reawaken to your soul, to the spiritual essence of who you really are.

If you are currently experiencing pain in your own life, I encourage you to look within to your soul and ask, "What can I learn from this? How can I grow through it?" If you slow yourself down, and if you allow yourself to become quiet, the voice of your soul will give you the answers you long to hear.

I pray that you may have seen a reflection of yourself in the words of this book, and that you were perhaps reawakened to the messages that were in it for you. Since the inspiration for this book was from God's Divine Spirit of love and light, it seems only fitting that the final thoughts come not from me, but through me:

I simply repeat once more…Open your eyes and look. Open your ears and listen. Open your heart and believe!

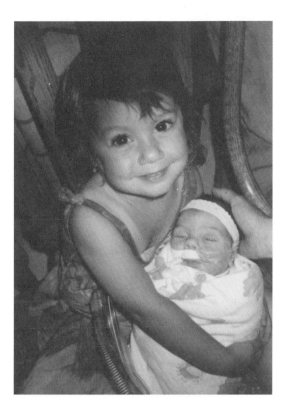

Ariana at 2½, proudly holding Talia

How to Contact Sandy Alemian-Goldberg

For information about Sandy's availability for speaking engagements, private soul coaching, or to share your own story of how you were reawakened spiritually, you can:

write:
LifeCraft
P.O. Box 301
E. Bridgewater, MA 02333

e-mail:
Sandy@seedsofhope.com

or

call us TOLL-FREE at 877-38-SEEDS

Please visit our website:
www.seedsofhope.com

We'd love to hear from you!

ORDER FORM

Please send _____ copy/copies of

Congratulations, It's an Angel at $14.95 each to:

Name: _____

Address: _____

_____

City/State/Zip: _____ / _____ / _____

Phone (_____) _____ - _____

E-mail address: _____

AMOUNT DUE:

_____ Copy/Copies at $14.95 ea. $_____

MA residents add 5% sales tax   _____

Shipping & handling

   First book $3.00   _____

   Additional books add $1.00 ea   _____

TOTAL ENCLOSED $_____

Please make checks or money orders payable to:

LifeCraft
P.O. Box 301
East Bridgewater, MA 02333

Or call TOLL-FREE 877-38-SEEDS
Major Credit Cards Accepted

Thank you very much for your order.